COMPACT LIVING

How to Design
Small Interior Space

Michael Guerra

 Permanent Publications

Published by

Permanent Publications
Hyden House Ltd
The Sustainability Centre
East Meon
Hampshire GU32 1HR
England
Tel: 01730 823 311
Fax: 01730 823 322
Overseas: (international code +44 - 1730)
Email: enquiries@permaculture.co.uk
Web: www.permaculture.co.uk

Designed by Two Plus George, www.TwoPlusGeorge.co.uk

Printed in the UK by Cambrian Printers, Aberystwyth, Wales

All paper from FSC certified mixed sources

FSC
www.fsc.org
MIX
Paper from
responsible sources
FSC® C005094

The Forest Stewardship Council (FSC) is a non-profit international
organisation established to promote the responsible management of the
world's forests. Products carrying the FSC label are independently certified
to assure consumers that they come from forests that are managed to meet
the social, economic and ecological needs of present and future generations.

British Library Cataloguing-in-Publication Data
A catalogue record for this book is available from the British Library

ISBN 978 1 85623 105 3

CONTENTS

The planet can give of itself only so much at a time; so it is beholden on us to use wisely what it can give sustainably. The planet does not care one way or another whether one species survives or not; it's been there many times before. However, as humans, genetically pre-disposed to care for our young so our genes are transmitted from one generation to the next, we inevitably become wholly concerned with the life our children will have; so it is important that we give them the tools to see wisely how to live wisely, so hopefully they can live happily.

ABOUT THE AUTHOR

Michael Guerra is a design engineer and sustainability consultant. Projects he has worked on include train, eco-house and railway station design, as well as working with Dr Ken Yeang on Building Integrated Food Production. He is currently engaged in a major green transport project which will allow overnight trains to run from London into Europe, paving the way for a more sustainable alternative to aviation travel.

Michael is also a permaculture designer, specialising in small urban designs, and is author of the bestselling book *The Edible Container Garden* published by Octopus.

Most importantly, Michael is a husband to Julia and father to Xavier, Alejandro and Joaquin, with whom he shares a very compact house and edible garden which has been sought out by people from more than a dozen countries. Michael spends his few free moments worrying about the future his sons will inherit whilst listening to them playing music (beautifully). Before reaching this point in his life Michael benefited from the experience of 26 different jobs (and between bouts of further education), leaving him with a 'jack of all trades', self-reliant approach to life with an openness to ideas which he hopes the reader will adopt. His mother worried that his listless approach to employment would mean that he would amount to nothing, but he is much happier for not following a direct course from cradle to grave in some grey office, as life is a journey, not a destination.

PREFACE

Whether we live in cities and towns or in the countryside our homes and gardens are getting smaller. In 1950 only a third of the world's population lived in urban environments. By 2025 this figure is predicted to rise to 60%. In parts of the world that are industrialising, this shift is driven by the movement of people away from their traditional villages and into cities and towns, seeking employment and a better life. Inevitably, urban space is at a premium and homes are by necessity smaller. In the West too, urban lifestyles make similar demands and the spaces in which we live and bring up families are shrinking whilst there is no sign of property prices falling. London, for instance, has never seen such buoyant property prices. Yet the squeeze is on rural homes too. As land and house prices increase, our homes and gardens are shrinking.

The world over, the conventional aspirational dream is for a big house surrounded by all the trappings of wealth – a seemingly endless collection of 'stuff' we don't really need. Yet what this really means for most people is higher mortgage payments, longer working hours, higher taxes and insurance, higher maintenance and cleaning costs, higher utility bills and more rooms to furnish. It is time to question our conventional aspirations and to ask, "What do we really want?" Do we want greater social status or greater freedom? Longer working weeks or more adventures? Happy and intimate relationships with family and friends or a triple garage full of expensive new toys? A low impact, green lifestyle or a fossil fuel guzzling one?

This book is written for anyone who is dissatisfied with the mantra of excessive materialism and for those who want to free themselves from crippling mortgage repayments. It is for anyone who wants to simplify their life, free themselves and have some fun. It has arisen from my own personal experience and is the story of how my family of five have lived a well designed yet very compact life in a small, one bedroom maisonette. What began as a financial necessity has become a way of life, affording us the freedom to explore our hobbies, artistic and musical leanings, growing food on the vertical as well as the horizontal, and travel throughout Europe by train.

I am not someone who enjoys DIY; I merely treat it as a matter of necessity, as we choose not to hire expertise. However, I do like designing because I like problem solving. I am, by profession, a design engineer. I survived university education with a degree or two, but that is less important than the many life experiences I have had, whilst trying to keep my head above water. Things like learning to cook from my mother (which really helped when I needed to work in restaurant kitchens); picking up a working knowledge of a few languages (which really helped in when driving big lorries across Europe – again from my linguist mother); and having an open heart (thanks to a friend along the way) made it possible for me to see the world in a new way and be open to all the possibilities of life. However, my greatest experience is the continuing one of parenthood, where I have been exceptionally fortunate in choice of partner and gift of children. It has forced me to rediscover the joys of innocence and see things anew, unfiltered, through bright eyes. It also brings back memories of the trials of education, as I try and help my children with their homework; all those things I thought I had forgotten finally becoming useful.

So, in writing this preface, I want to thank my beautiful family for their forbearance, their patience, and perhaps some understanding of the bearded guy who grasps them too tightly when they return home from school. I really love you so much. I only hope that you will inherit a world you deserve.

INTRODUCTION

At the time of writing this book the UK Government had announced that it intends to allow the building of over one million additional houses, mostly in the crowded southeast, with a good number on floodplain or on prime agricultural land. This is driven by the breaking up of households into smaller units, the magnetic economic draw of London and its hinterland, and increasing aspirational pressure on society to conform to the Western model of consumption economics. The UK population is not increasing markedly, merely that the demographic is changing. All this is clearly unsustainable. As the agricultural footprint of London increases, the availability of viable agricultural land decreases, along with its service population. In Cuba, where the loss of Soviet oil has severely dented the economy since 1989, they have taken radical steps to grow food in cities; within parks and empty building lots. In the world's oil dependent nations this state of emergency will be arriving all too soon. Obviously, a change to edible landscaping can alleviate some of the agricultural shortfall, but if the landscape is buried under concrete it will not happen.

The issue of property ownership is worth mentioning here. This book was written during a time when property is seen as the only thing of value, and prices have escalated to many times the average wage. Because of this people do not have enough money to put into a pension or other investment, so the property they struggle to afford will have to serve as capital for their retirement, often instead of being seen as an asset to leave to their children. In 2008 there began a global economic crisis, which was due to the domino effect of banks buying debt from other banks (so seemingly spreading risk), and then that debt investment failing as people were unable to afford the over-inflated mortgages they had taken out to provide for their retirement. As people are living longer, there is greater pressure to maximise their investment so that they can enjoy their retirement (because they didn't enjoy their working lives which was stressed by paying off the big mortgage). There is less room to build new houses, and as each house is valued on its structural size (the garden having little relative value), ever larger houses are being built on ever smaller pieces of land. People see property development as

The mainstream aspiration of a big consumptive house occupying ever diminishing green spaces are a key mechanism in the acceleration of the human population towards unsustainability.

a relatively easy way of making money, resulting in the inflation of house prices. There is also a pressure on people to 'improve' their investment by building extensions into the ever smaller gardens. As gardens disappear, so does our chance at sustainability. We need to break the cycle of ever more concrete. It does not take much imagination to realise that in a post-oil economy a large house with a small garden, with its attendant increased running costs, will become a financial liability, whereas a small house with a large garden will be seen as a sustaining asset.

This book was written in a small, ground floor maisonette with one bedroom. The house is home to a happy family of five. The mortgage has been paid off. There are fruit, vegetables and herbs growing in the small garden. Perhaps not enough to fully sustain the family, but enough to ensure that something fresh can be tasted everyday of the year. It started off as a matter of accident, then a matter of necessity; eventually becoming logical, practical and normal. We live in London's hinterland surrounded by big houses, big cars and other aspirational nonsense. Most of the big houses are empty during the week as their inhabitants commute to their long hours in the City, trying to earn enough to support their huge mortgages. Dear Reader, if you are one of these, please do not be offended if I think you are mad!

Compact living can be a matter of necessity, or a lifestyle choice. It is a practical alternative to expansive living; it can be a positive experience, and it has major implications for a sustainable future.

Western economies are driven by a need to sell stuff that people generally don't need, and generally ends up in landfill. Break the chain and temper your psychological need to accumulate. Does the stuff that you don't use have a value you could recoup, or could someone else use it? Lighten the load. If you do need something new, make sure that it fulfils your need. Buy for multi-use, durability and maintainability. Are you a family with children? Do you really need an executive five bedroom house (with double garage and no garden) – or is that a recipe for mortgage stress and family alienation?

> **Think smaller, borrow less, and talk to your family more during the extra hours you don't have to be at work; you never know, you might actually like each other!**

While this book was not written as a self-help manual, it is important that before embarking on compact living you ask yourself whether happiness is a function of how much stuff you have (or are seen to have)? Do you take an unhealthy interest in celebrity culture? Are you preoccupied by how others see you; would your friends understand if you chnaged your lifestyle?

By breaking the chain of stuff accumulation, you will also be embarking on a philosophical journey into the unknown. While not quite full blown Buddhism it is also quite liberating; your resources will not be so stretched, you will be less stressed, and you will have more time to attend to the important things in life, like your friends and family.

Many people go through periods when compact living is an imperative, rather than a choice. Leaving home and living in rented rooms for a job, going to university, or downsizing when the children have left home will always focus the mind on the real necessities of life. All such situations can be unsettling; leaving the security of home when beginning one's independence, or having to go through all life's accumulations at the end of a long life when the finances will no longer support a larger space: at some point we all have to face up to the inevitable.

However, don't fret; the practicalities of compact living are really straightforward, as are the early stages to achieve it. You can treat it as no more intense than a particularly thorough spring clean. Do as much or as little as you have time for. Be honest with yourself, and if possible do it with a friend.

My family and I have lived compactly together for over twenty years. There have been growing pains, a few trying decisions and more than a few discussions with small persons about why their friends have bigger houses, and equally why their friends don't seem to have very exciting holidays (every Easter we take long train rides across the world). It has required some practical design skills, and more than one Christmas holiday cleaning sawdust off every surface in the house! We often wonder if we can maintain it for much longer as our children grow ever larger. We have a particular problem with guitars – a burgeoning talent of the eldest – and we are aware of the middle child's desire to play drums (fortunately the youngest only needs a saxophone!). But despite the challenges, we are happy, busy, and never tire of each other's company.

Most of the world's population does not live in suburban splendour, surrounded with mown lawns, carports and air conditioning. Indeed much of the world's population is struggling to survive while the 'first world' benefit from their desperation. From a moral standpoint it is hard to support our Western lifestyle, from a logical point of view it is a sustainability non-starter. Yet the means of living a happy, high quality life is all around us, without having to deny our children's future or those whose accident of birth means that they will be lucky to see out their childhood. What is required is a change of focus from Quantity to Quality, from Aspiration to Need. In a conversation with a banker's wife she explained that the mindset of many wealthier friends was that they strived to earn a lot of money in order to ignore the consequences of global warming, the end of oil and the impact of unsustainable farming practices. They live in their big houses or sit in their big 4x4 cars blithely ignoring the end of the world by ensuring that they will always have enough. Obviously, not a good attitude if we are to avoid extinction. Yet these people are held as aspirational models for many people, which perhaps is even scarier. With freedom come responsibilities and if we are to survive beyond the end of this century then those who *have* will need to take responsibility for those who *have not*. In permaculture parlance, we need to change our global philosophy to Earthcare, Peoplecare and Fair Shares.

CHAPTER 1 | Think Small, Think Happy

It is not the place of this book to tell you how to be happy. It is something that is experienced within and cannot be imposed from without. We are bombarded enough with advertisers telling us that purchasing a certain product will improve our lifestyle or make us happy. At best, falling for their tag line will lighten our lives temporarily while permanently lightening our pockets. However, in order to accept change to a more compact life, it is important that a certain amount of happy supplication is required.

When we are born we emerge with not much more than a smile. We are given everything we need, we are cleaned and dressed and carried around by our parents. In different cultures that need can be fulfilled with equipment as basic as a piece of fabric and a mother's breast, or in the other extreme a 4-wheel drive people mover, an off-road pram, an expensive wardrobe and a full-time nursemaid. It could be argued the baby that is carried around at the mother's breast is happier than the one that is constantly kept at arms' length in various modes of transport. This is, of course, an extreme example, but emphasises the way innocence is soon lost and how we use stuff accumulation not to mark important stages of our lives, but to fill the emptiness of lost innocence. It is a difficult cycle to break.

This chapter is about changing the mindset of domestic living. From a simplistic sustainability point of view the less land we use for housing, the more land there would be to grow food, and for wildlife, on which our agriculture mostly depends. If we could grow more food where we live then less of it would have to come from far way, so saving natural resources. Western economies are starting to wake up to the implications of a life without oil. We use it for everything. There is more oil used for food than you could possibly imagine; for fertilisers, pest control, ploughing, cropping, shipping, processing, packaging and then more transport, before anyone drives to the mega-market to buy it. Take away oil and what do you have? Starvation or the necessity of grow your own. It is this realisation that makes compact living implicit, not by

What are food miles?

Food miles are the distance your food has to travel to get from the grower to your plate.

Check food labels for country of origin!

Food miles Easterfield 2010: A wonderful poster produced for Transition Ireland depicting the environmental price paid for food that is not produced where it is needed.

forcing more of us to live closer together in pods, but by using less land for housing so that we have more land left to provide for our needs.

Many more of us are forced into compact living than would choose it. As a species we probably started on the open plains of Africa, and there may still be some genetic pre-disposition to living unhindered by walls. Plains hunter-gatherers would live very lightly, carrying everything they need on their back or on a small sledge. Their culture is carried around in their heads, with stories repeated from generation to generation. Similarly, nomadic cultures which follow the supply of food for their domesticated animals manage to carry everything they need from place to place, often to pack their entire household, including the house, in a matter of hours. No room for excess baggage.

In the West, baggage and space are more psychological issues than issues of real need. The old question of what you would try to save in the event of fire should be repeated here. What things do you have that are so tied to your life that you could not live without them? How much space do you need to live? Do you really need to be able to swing a cat? Would the cat mind?

It is interesting to note that different cultures respond differently to those questions, and have different approaches to compact spatial living.

Tokyo suburb: These suburbs are far more densely zoned than in Europe and North America. No space for rolling lawns, swimming pools or double garages. Space is, however, made for the dead. This cemetery (top right) sits between apartment blocks. The Kyoto street view (top left) shows that most electrical and communication infrastructure is above ground, due to the threat of earthquakes.

Tokyo night: Tokyo is a typical megacity where most of the population live in tiny apartments, generally only half the size of comparable accommodation in Europe or North America.

7

Japan is always noted for the self-discipline of its people. The reasons are probably historical, and based upon the hierarchy within society; but the reasons are also geographic. Japan is a mountainous country, with most of the population crowded on to the narrow coastal plains. As nearly all economic activity is concentrated in this area and land prices are very high, it forces everyone into smaller volumes. Without commensurate levels of social respect and self-discipline Japan would be a scary chaotic place. Living at such densities has forced the Japanese to think creatively about how they use space, as well the physical dimensions of everything they use in the house. It is also probably no coincidence that Japan is the birthplace of the personal stereo.

In approaching the mindset required to be happy within a compact household you have to ask yourself the basic questions: Quality of Life vs. Quantity of Stuff; Aspiration vs. Need. For most people these are difficult questions to answer because they find it difficult to distinguish between Quality and Quantity, or between Aspiration and Need. However most people would be able to resolve the difference between a rushed fast food meal and one that was cooked with care at home. Monetarily, there would be little difference between the two, but the level of satisfaction is worlds apart. Similarly, most people understand the difference between the developing world needing clean drinking water and aspiring to bottled fizzy drinks. (This is perhaps not such a good example as in some places in the world the penetration of some global corporations has meant that the only safe water to drink is a well known addictive carbonated beverage.)

Coca-cola in Ethiopia: Many corporations are investing in developing countries, not to improve living conditions and sustainable water and sanitation, but to develop markets for their addictive products.

Compact living does not necessarily mean living as an ascetic. While living with the privations of a monk or hermit is very cheap, it is not for everyone, though many people I know could use the experience! Asceticism requires a particular self-discipline; a mild version will be required in **The Battle with Stuff**.

CHAPTER 2

Stuff, and The Battle To Control It

As anyone that has had to clear out a deceased relative's home knows, stuff can be both a menace and a joy. Sorting through the remains of someone's life can be emotional, as well as hard physical labour. The great piles of paper, pictures, odd souvenirs, little decorations, books, videos, music, furniture, kitchen equipment all seem too much. And yet these day-to-day items had meaning or some use to someone at some time. Whilst undertaking this task, you inevitably think of all things you have accumulated at home that you have never made time to sort through.

As you go methodically through each room, you have to decide what to do with every item. Hopefully there was a will made, so any special items will have been left to specific people. In any case, when clearing a house, it is important to make sure that everyone (e.g. all the children of the deceased) go through the house together and list specific objects that have meaning to them. Gentle acquiescence is a good trait to have through these difficult times! Sorting through your own stuff can be equally trying. It is important to note that although you see the stuff as your own, ownership is only temporary, as you will be passing it on in the fullness of time.

So how do you start? Living as a family will mean that most stuff will have meaning or has been used by more than one member of the family. It is important that every member of the family understands the process and will be involved in the sorting. This can be difficult as not everyone may be as committed, but being non-committal does not mean they should not have a say. As our household has been compact from the outset, so the children accept that they will grow out of toys, books and clothes. They know that without recycling old toys, new ones will not appear on birthdays or Christmas (though to be honest, many of their 'new' toys had a previous life). There are things, which have sentimental or practical value that might serve another generation, and for those things there is Deep Store. It is useful for each member of the family to make lists of those things that are important or useful to them. That will

Charity Shops are an ideal place to recycle any items that could be used by someone else, but perhaps are not worth the bother of trying to sell.

provide a check prior to any item permanently leaving the building.

If you live alone, the process is perhaps easier, though it is a lonely business. It is better to invite a friend round for the afternoon, and over cups of tea and cake sort through a room. It is often the case that they may be able to use some of your cast-offs, so saving you a trip to the charity shop or recycling centre. And you could also return the favour and offer to help them sort out their stuff.

Doctors use the term 'triage' to describe the sorting process of patients in an hospital Accident and Emergency department. Patients are sorted into those requiring emergency treatment, those without a life-threatening condition, and those whom treatment would not help. While sorting your stuff is unlikely to be quite so traumatic, primary sorting will require the making of three piles: Everyday, Deep Store and Out. Each of these piles in turn will have to be sub-sorted, but for now it is important to focus on the triage.

Arm yourself with pen and paper, sticky labels and a number of boxes and bags. You can start anywhere you want, but just do one room at a time. Make sure you have a clear space in which to work within the room. Turn off the phone, turn on some music and make a cup of tea. Methodically work from one end of the room to the other. Clear the wardrobes first, then the drawers and finally any odd corners or suitcases. Divide the contents of each container into three piles: Everyday, Deep Store and Out. Try and keep the piles neat and check items for damage: it will have a bearing on whether it is worth keeping, selling, taking to a charity shop, or recycling.

There are some really good books on recycling and where you can take stuff so that someone else can reuse it. Also check out eBay if you think something may be valuable, but do not forget to equate your time, as you may spend hours preparing something for auction and then only get 99p for it. Also check out www.freecycle.org for a really good way of recycling something locally. Most household waste centres in the UK have areas that can recycle a huge range of items beyond the normal glass, metal, paper and plastic. Most will take such household items as fridges, furniture, computer equipment, electrical equipment etc. But before we get to that stage ask the following questions about the items you are sorting:

CLOTHES AND SHOES

Do you need it? Does it fit you? Is it in a reasonable condition? Would you wear it everyday/week? – if 'Yes' to all those questions then put it in the Everyday pile. If 'No' to the last question then put it in Deep Store. If 'No' to any of the other questions then it goes to the Out pile.

PAPERWORK

You will need to make decisions about old tax records, receipts, bills, etc. It is good to have them organised, and even better to have this stuff recorded on a computer spreadsheet, or double-entry book, but the reality is that we rarely have the time. So unless you have always organised your finances well it is probably only really necessary to keep the stuff from the last six years. Make sure that you file it in envelopes or files on a year-by-year basis. With other official paperwork, like copies of deeds, wills, etc. make sure you have it all sorted. With old correspondence (love letters, etc.) and birthday cards it is up to you. Do you want your children to read them, do you think they will have historic significance? In our house we like keeping old postcards and stamps from interesting places, but that is because we have a geographic interest. For anything in the Out pile, shred and recycle it.

ELECTRICAL

Old electrical equipment needs to be treated with care. Very few charitable organisations will accept even nearly new equipment. Some equipment

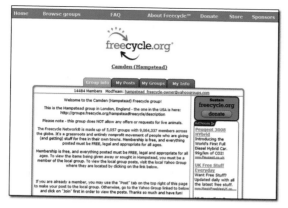

Freecycle: An alternative to charity shops and eBay, for those items which may be either too big or too unusual.

has a residual value (especially old valve guitar amps) and they are worth repairing or refurbishing by an expert. If something no longer works, and neither you nor anyone else can repair it and use it then it needs to be broken up and recycled. Newer equipment is more likely to separate into component parts and materials that can be recycled. In any case don't dump it, get it recycled. Computer equipment is a particular problem as it is outmoded quite quickly. If a machine is less than three or four years old it is probably worth taking it to a place that sends it to the developing world. Make sure that you completely scrub the hard disk for any personal data (there is specialist software for this, as simply re-formatting does not work).

DECORATIVE

For those of you who like to live in a constant state of Victorian clutter, Stop! I've been to so many houses (bigger of course) where the occupants have filled the space with meaningless decorative figurines, plates, and cheesy pictures. They say nothing about your life (except your taste) and stop you from using that space more effectively. It may be that some of this clutter has meaning to you, by all means keep the items that say something positive about your life, or may have meaning to the next generation. For the other stuff, recycle it.

FURNITURE

Recycling old furniture is far more difficult today due to regulations on fire safety. The problems are more acute with padding, fabrics and plastics, so if the item is irreparable then it will have to be broken up and recycled as best you can. Softwood furniture often has to be protected with a special varnish (not nice) that chars rather than allowing a flame to take hold. Old hardwood furniture is often worth repairing; it will burn, but the dense nature of a timber like oak means that it does so more slowly. When buying furniture, do think of what can be done with it at the end of its life: we have successfully composted two all-cotton futons in the garden (they take nine to twelve months to break down when mixed with other garden waste).

MISCELLANEOUS FABRIC

If you are slightly handy you can always make new out of old. Unfortunately, some fabrics get so worn that they are too frail even for rag. You could try your hand at papermaking, or making felt, but if that is beyond you all natural fabrics can be commercially recycled, and even some manmade fibres can now be reused.

TOOLS

Most hand tools, if they are well looked-after and maintained, can be used for generations. A wipe down with a lightly oiled rag after use is all that is usually required. Unfortunately, even the hardest screwdriver can get notched and damaged, and if it is beyond sharpening or repair then it will need to be recycled.

KITCHEN EQUIPMENT

You can never have enough teaspoons! However, you can have too many fondue sets. It may be surprising how little kitchen equipment you actually need. Recycle anything you haven't used for more than a year. You may also wish to review you crockery and cutlery requirements, certainly there is little room for a fully loaded Welsh Dresser in a compact house. If you don't use it, lose it.

CHEMICALS

Old pots of paint and varnish are best taken to the household waste site for proper disposal. Your future decorating requirements will not need

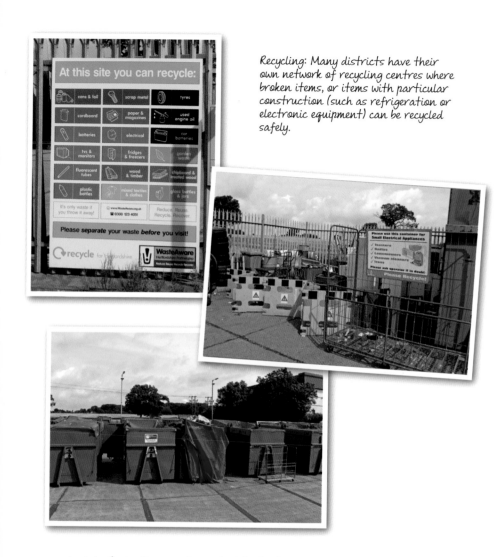

Recycling: Many districts have their own network of recycling centres where broken items, or items with particular construction (such as refrigeration or electronic equipment) can be recycled safely.

materials that off-gas solvent inside the house. Also look carefully at all the cleaners and detergents that clutter up your cupboards, while they may remove limescale and stains, think about what they may be doing to your skin and brain.

MEDICINES

Any unused medicines should be taken back to the nearest chemist.

Eventually you will be left with a small treasure chest, a change of clothes for winter and summer, a backpack, a knife, fork and spoon, a plate, a sleeping bag and a small stove. Oh yes, and an empty house! Seriously though, you should have found everything you thought you have lost, and you should have cleaned every room in the house.

With the stuff in the Out pile you will need to further sort it into stuff that can be Sold, Reused, Repaired and Recycled.

Among the items that you have decided to keep will be things that have real meaning to your life. Personal letters, photographs, odd souvenirs from a life of travel, inherited antiques, diaries, etc. These are your treasures. Have a look at them and decide whether they are in good condition, whether they need repair, and ask yourself how precious they are to you. Do you need to have them around you, to see and to touch, or are they objects you can archive and store, safe in the knowledge that you can always get them out when you want to. Or are the objects so precious, especially to your family, that they need to be kept in a bank deposit. Such things could often serve as emergency finance in times of desperate need, but if not used can be passed to the next generation.

You will have to decide yourself what you want to keep in your treasure box. But when you have decided, along with everything else you are keeping, it is time to decide what is **Everyday** and what is **Deep Store**.

EARLY FLATS

© Heath Robinson
& K.R.G. Browne

15

CHAPTER 3

Everyday Stuff vs Deep Store (The Practicalities)

In every normal domestic situation there are things that you use everyday (kettle, teapot, teaspoon, mug, underwear) and things that get used only on a seasonal basis (winter coat, Christmas decorations, sunscreen). The frequency with which you use an item will determine how easy it should be to get out. In our household we Deep Store our seasonal clothes, and around the first of November and the first of April the great change happens. The heavy fleeces and sweaters, thermal underwear, heavy duvets and heavy coats are compressed in clean bags and Deep Stored in April, while a much smaller selection of thin blouses, shorts, skirts, etc. are packed away in November.

Taking each room in turn:

KITCHEN

In the kitchen, certain equipment is kept out all the time. We cook a lot, so the cutting boards, knives, mixer and food processor are always available for use. The ice-cream maker and juicer are less frequently used and so are stored in shelves under work surfaces. Tea mugs are out, while the best china tea service is in a cupboard. Our kitchen is compact, though not quite as compact as a train kitchen. It is extraordinary to think that from a 2mx2.5m kitchen it is possible to produce three courses for fifty to a hundred people. Of course, it depends on considerable discipline and preparation, but living in a small space demands a less lazy approach to kitchen use. 'Clean and clear as you go', my mother used to cry when teaching me to cook. There is, of course, equipment that will probably get very little use, but needs to be accessible at all times, and in a position that is clearly visible at all times – First Aid and Fire Safety equipment. Statistically the most dangerous room in a house is the kitchen, and that is where you should store your plasters, burn cream and bandages in a clearly marked container. Similarly, every kitchen should have a fire blanket near the stove; it is sobering to think that spilling a few tablespoons of water into a cupful of boiling oil can cause a 4m ball of flame, enough to engulf a kitchen in a couple of seconds. Being such a source of potential danger it is important that you should review your kitchen layout with respect of identifying and reducing risk. A full health and safety inspection may seem a little ridiculous, but if you are to operate in your kitchen in confidence you should ensure that you have a good clear space to prep with good lighting to avoid digit dismemberment, that you do not store flammable objects next to the stove, and that you always have a clear path between the stove and the sink in case of emergency.

BATHROOM

The bathroom is an everyday room, and it may seem that there would not be much division between things you use every day and things that are only used occasionally, but depending on the size of your bathroom it could be used far more efficiently. People usually store their medicines in the bathroom, yet that is not where you should keep your First Aid kit (see kitchen above). A bathroom is the most humid room, and therefore is not a good place to store books (though some people do – though a toilet cubicle is better). Without efficient ventilation paper can soon start to rot making a bathroom a poor place for a second library. If your bathroom is large enough you could deep-store linen, your spare bedclothes, towels and out-of-season clothes in compressible airtight bags (the ones with a valve, which when you roll them up forces all the air out). Put the bags in a shelved floor to ceiling corner cupboard; it will make your bathroom smaller, but you can always fix towel rails to the outside; and besides how much room do you actually need to ablute? If, however, you have built yourself a Japanese-style wet room, any wooden storage is inadvisable (tiled surfaces are the norm).

BEDROOM

A bedroom in a compact house is just another multi-purpose space with a folding bed in it. Generally though, it is where your clothes are more likely to be stored. You should have sorted your clothes into seasonal piles, with a central pile of everyday items. Put your everyday items in easy access drawers, pack away your out-of-season clothes in compressible bags. Your in-season clothes can be stored in the seasonal-access drawers

Corner storage used for toys, books and clothes in crates.

and hanging spaces. Hopefully, you will only have kept those clothes you actually need and so storage will be far easier.

For some people compact living is considered a retrograde step in their lives, something to be ashamed of and which somehow always seems temporary. Much of that is a reflection on a Western attitude to success, which is more about visible acquisition aspiration, rather than considered happiness or peace of mind. Such emotions can be a barrier to moving on or of finding a new place in the world. While it is clearly a psychological rather than a physical need, such feelings can often be deflected by some considered storage. It can be quite traumatic if circumstances force you to move from one comfortable situation to a more compressed space where all your stuff won't fit. The feeling of displacement can be over-powering and it is important that you regain some sense of self in your new surroundings. This is not always a simple thing, but quite often it is simply a matter of focusing on those items which have the greatest meaning and providing a safe, but visible, place to put them while you go through the various stages of downsizing. Some people describe having their sanity protected by seemingly quite arbitrary objects, though family pictures are usual.

SITTING ROOM

If you have a separate sitting room (or day room) then you are living more expansively than we are! What would have been the sitting room in a 'normal' one bedroom flat is a multi-functional bedroom/library/dining room/office. It is the room where we spend the most time together as a family during the hours of daylight. As such, nearly everything in this room is for everyday access: books, video media, music, etc. There are a couple of less accessible corners where we do keep some Deep Store archives, but the rest of the room is arranged for instant accessibility.

While Deep Store is the obvious location for items that have little everyday practical value, and a treasure box is a good location for precious personal items, there are some objects that make any place 'home' and so need special consideration. Make time to place these special objects. You might find that having them visible will make the transition easier to bear.

It is often the case that when moving into more compact accommodation there is simply too little room to accommodate cherished large objects of furniture, pictures,

Crates and hanging rail used for clothes, upper shelves for camping equipment.

etc., or you have to suddenly rescue a large number of items from a relative or friend who can no longer look after them for you. If you do not have time to perform an organised triage then you will need to move everything into temporary storage. This is less cost-effective than sorting everything properly, but sometimes life doesn't give you the opportunity. A couple of times I've had to hire a 7.5T truck (we haven't had a car since 1987) and trundle around finding homes for my mother's accumulated furnishings. Not much fun.

Rented storage can range from borrowing space in a friend's garage, renting a council or commercial lock-up garage, to renting space in a commercial secure warehouse. The problem with this is that once stored it becomes a matter of 'out of sight, out of mind', and it becomes all too easy to defer the fateful event. This is obviously a decision of last resort, and should not be undertaken lightly.

CHAPTER 4

Zoned Multi-Spaces for You and Your Stuff

On our long railway adventures we often take sleeper trains. The carriages are fitted out with sleeping compartments, each one having seating that converts into beds at night. They are a perfect practical example of a multifunctional small space.

Providing that you have organised your rooms efficiently there is no reason why the function of a particular space cannot be changed in a minute or two. In our small flat almost every room has more than one function. The Hall is tiny (2.5 x 1m) so there is really only room for the hanging of coats. The bathroom (1.8 x 1.8m) is also small, but it is used as a private phone booth (using a cordless phone).

It would seem that with estate agents' preoccupation with numbers of bedrooms and en-suite bathrooms that we spend most of our lives either asleep or on the toilet! And yet what are these rooms used for when the occupants are not sleeping or abluting? It costs money to maintain these rooms for most of the day, in terms of mortgage interest and maintenance

In what would be the bedroom (2.4m x 3.5m) in a one bedroom flat we accommodate the three children's beds, storage for clothes, children's books and toys, a folding desk, a couple of folding foam chairs and a TV. It works on the principle that when it is time to sleep the beds are out and occupy the majority of the room. When it is time to do homework the beds are folded away and the folding desk is deployed; and when it is time to play the floor space is cleared.

In what would normally be a sitting room is a folding futon double-bed, a multi-functional table that is used for dining, working and storage, shelving storage on three walls (the fourth wall looks out onto the back garden), and an office corner that includes a computer, printer, scanner and file drawers. This room is our sitting room, double bedroom, dining room, office, library, music room and entertainment room. It takes just a few moments to convert from one function to another.

The kitchen also functions as a workshop for small dust-free jobs. A small vice can be clamped to the worktop to allow for repairing or soldering small items. A mobile tool chest is stored under the work surface and for larger projects we have a folding workbench that is set up in the garden.

Students have to think of how best to set out their study-bedrooms when in confining accommodation in halls of residence. They often have to share facilities or their rooms. Rules develop that seek to keep the peace and to ensure a fair division of simple maintenance tasks (like washing up!). A space-efficient household has to operate in the same way, otherwise chaos ensues, and leaving everyone embittered by the experience.

Living in multi-functional spaces requires some discipline from inception of design to daily use, especially if the space is shared.

'La vida es sueño' or 'life is a dream', as my ancestor Pedro Calderón de la Barca wrote in 1635. Although not directly related to the trials of Segismundo, any design project requires a period of reflection and 'virtual' planning. It is important that if the room is to work then due consideration is given to how the various components are to function within the space and the order in which the components are deployed.

To make a room multi-functional it is important to keep as much free space in the centre as possible to allow sufficient room for safe movement and to avoid hurting anyone when something heavy is dropped or slid into use. Classically a multi-functional room has all the paraphernalia arranged around the perimeter of the room. In our main dayroom we started by designing 300mm deep shelves from floor to ceiling on three sides. This was then penetrated by first the sofa-bed, then the DVD cabinet, the TV and the computer corner. We designed a mobile storage table that provides some storage for bedclothes etc. with folding sides to allow eating on or doing homework.

In the children's bedroom the space was defined by folding bunks. The logic is simple: if you want to sleep then the beds come out, if you want to play or do homework then beds are folded away to the wall. The children have been on dozens of night trains and are well used to the discipline, and they are close enough in age to have the same bedtime. You will see from the pictures that we have fixed a folding table to the underside of the bottom bed.

Many people define themselves by their hobby. A great many people practise their hobbies at home and in special rooms. My mother always wanted a sewing room, and in one of the houses we lived in she

Main day room ...

assembled all her paraphernalia in a spare bedroom; sewing machine, embroidery frames, drawers and cupboards of materials. There were a couple of occasional beds in the corner and a large folding table. For a year it was her pride, but soon the embroidery frame was in the sitting room, and when the sewing machine was used it was carried down to the dining room. Very soon the sewing room had reverted to being the spare bedroom. At the same time my father had extended the house to include a sizeable library. This was to be where he would keep and repair his collection of ancient leather-bound books. He had set up a small workshop in the corner dedicated to his hobby of bookbinding. Within a year, however, he was back working on the wobbly dining room table. The reason: the TV was in the dining room.

A friend asked me a while back if I could advise on the design of a shed or extension where she could do her graphic design (which she does for a living). She also produces engraved and etched glassware for sale, working in a separate workroom and there is a sewing room in her

... with corner office opened.

... ready for lunch.

... as cinema.

... as bedroom.

... ready for homework.

... with bed half unfolded.

... with one of the model railways lowered
from the ceiling on to the table.

... as recording studio.

sizeable cottage which she shares with her husband and two children. Her husband has a small barn at the end of the garden for 'projects'. I suggested that she might consider using her sewing room as a multi-functional hobby space, equip it with some entertainment, and therefore could do any work that takes her fancy. I explained that our office space is 0.8m wide, 0.6m deep and 2m high, and is large enough to take a large computer (with 24″ screen), a large flatbed scanner, a duplexing printer (prints both sides of the paper at once), and numerous drawers for A4 folders, computer disks, etc. She hadn't considered a multi-purpose space and has not spoken to me since!

Almost any room can be converted into another. The only real limitations are due to an incompatibility of health and safety issues. UK planning rules state that there should be two doors between an area where food is processed and a toilet. So despite the fact that both areas could share plumbing and ventilation, they should not be a shared space. That is to say that they could share a wall, but the two rooms should each have a door. This is sometimes difficult to achieve in some very compact designs, but it is a primary regulation. You should also avoid combining spaces of high dust and/or humidity with areas where computers or unprotected audio-visual equipment is to be used. While it is certainly possible to find waterproof radios and flat screen TVs now, avoid using your bathroom as an office. The same is also true for greenhouses or hot (equator-facing) conservatories; modern computer processors need a lot of cooling.

Give serious consideration as to how a piece of equipment is to be used when deployed. A computer with a separate screen and keyboard (i.e. not a lap or notebook) is better arranged to provide more comfortable ergonomics. To set the ideal height for working sit in the chair you plan to use for working (ensuring that it is comfortable and supportive), then measure the distance from the floor to the underside of your elbow. That distance will be the ideal height for your desk. If your desk slides out then make it 600mm deep and 850mm wide; that will give you enough space to operate a mouse and keyboard, while giving you knee room under the desk. Mount your screen at least 600mm away to save your eyes and set at a height and angle that is comfortable for your sitting position. The pull-out desk will need to have a cut-out in the middle 500mm wide and around 150mm deep so that your forearms are supported while you type or use the mouse (should you have a larger tummy then you might

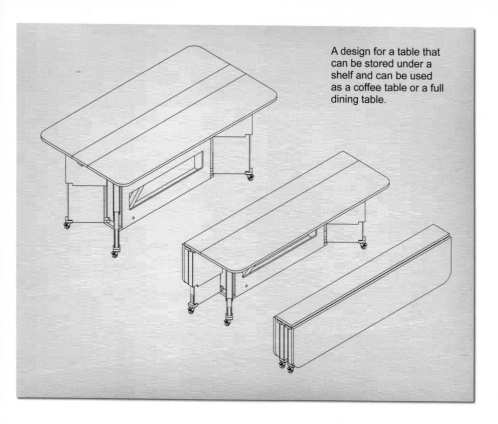

A design for a table that can be stored under a shelf and can be used as a coffee table or a full dining table.

need more room). Corner desks are ideal for working at a computer, but a little harder to make to slide out.

A sewing machine is a classic example of a heavy piece of equipment that you do not want to cart around from room to room. It is better to have it cantilever or slide out from a wall. All machines will need to have an extension on the left side to support your work, with room on the other side of the machine for the work move to freely beyond the machine. The shelf doesn't need to be very deep; perhaps only 50mm wider than the machine on either side, however it should be mounted at the same height as a desk. Pay attention to the lighting; most sewing machines come with a work light, but it is sometimes better to mount a moveable work light to the right of the machine (an LED on a flexible head is ideal).

Task lighting is something that often gets overlooked in multi-use spaces. Think about where your equipment is, how you are going to operate it, and how you want to light your work. Also think about whether you need a broad ambient light (for large work) or small focused light for small work. If you are working at a computer screen do not work in ambient darkness as you will struggle to see the keyboard, or your notes or books you are working from. Instead use a small directional light to shine on your work adjacent to the keyboard, or to shine on to light ceiling or wall next to you. Eye strain can be caused by excessive contrast, as well as excessive reflection on the screen; do not work at a computer with high-level fluorescent lights or sunlight reflecting on the screen – I learnt this lesson the hard way. We now use a number of flexible LED clip-mounted lights around the house for task lighting.

A modern bed-sitting-room

CHAPTER 5

Storage Principles & Ideas

'What', 'where' and 'how' are the storage questions you need to answer. Presuming that the items you are storing are things that have been carefully sorted from those things that you do not wish to keep (and presumably have gone to a happy life elsewhere), then you will be faced with a (smaller) pile of objects that you either use everyday, use occasionally, use seasonally or items you wish to archive as treasure or for tax purposes.

The basic principles of storage are to keep things safe, accessible and in loads that are easy to handle. Essentially you want to know where things are, know that they are safe, not have to empty your house to find them, and not end up in hospital after your search. Seems logical doesn't it?

The trouble is that we generally accumulate stuff over a period of time, not in organised bouts (except for that time when I came back from two years in the USA with a sizeable collection of records!). So in organising your stuff for storage you are making a conscious decision to plan for when new stuff finds its way through your defences into the house. This is important because, except for properly archived Deep Store items, all your other storage must be adaptable (and not so stuffed) so that new or differently sized replacements can be accommodated without having to go through a major sorting and repacking session.

You will be storing your stuff in a number of different ways:

- Shelves
- Cupboards
- Drawers
- Mobile boxes or cases
- Hanging on walls
- Hanging from ceilings
- Stackable boxes
- Any variation or combination of the above

If you ever get the opportunity, try and visit the Sir George Soane museum in London. This remarkable house was home to Sir George's art collection, and while the art itself may not be to everyone's taste, how it is housed and arranged is amazing. Imagine false walls and cupboards that open to reveal more art, mirrors to expand views and every nook and cranny filled with objects small and large.

Organising the kind of storage you need is fairly commonsense. Things you use everyday are kept handy on shelves, in drawers or in open cupboards at heights that do not require steps or a lot of bending down. Things that you only need occasionally are kept in boxes at less convenient heights. Convenience and safety is key. Daily access should be such that you can find things easily in the dark (e.g. during a power cut), or if you are tired or unwell. All your heavy items should be stored at waist height to reduce lifting from ground level, though it would be better if you do not have to lift them at all by putting them on wheels, or in drawers supported by heavy duty full extension slides.

SHELVES

We take many kinds of storage for granted. The technology is many thousands of years old, and yet even a simple shelf needs to have thought applied before it is installed.

Longitudinally a shelf is a beam. Depending on its construction, materials and loads it will deflect. This deflection is normal, and providing the stress in the material is less than the yield stress it will not break. How the shelf is supported also has a bearing on its performance. If the shelf is built from the floor up (e.g. supported on a frame or piles of bricks) then you need to think about whether the floor will take the weight. If your floor is solid concrete (or compressed earth) then you will only need to think about whether you mind a dent in the carpet. If your floor is floating (e.g. timber floorboards on joists or beams) then you will have to think about whether the wall supporting a heavy shelf is strong enough. Remember, we do not have to worry particularly if the shelf is going to support a few trinkets, but in compact living shelves are a primary form of storage of sometimes quite sizeable storage systems. Your shelves might be used for storing heavy crockery, books or old vinyl records, all of which have a greater density than the timber the shelves are made of.

Deep bookshelves above sofa. Note steel angle used as a sliding picture rail, a small collection of souvenirs, and note flexible LED lamp.

Heavy shelving should not be supported off a wall, whatever its construction, though fixing to the wall is recommended to stabilise the shelves. A simple timber plank shelf can be supported in a number of ways. The way we usually do it is to construct ladder frames from timber that rest on the floor and are fixed to the plasterboard walls to stop them from falling over. The shelves themselves then rest on the ladder frames. Different areas can be compartmentalised or enclosed for different functions, or can support fully extending drawers or rolling storage. Over time you may wish to adapt your storage for different functions as your family arrangement changes, or perhaps your mobility and access needs change. The trick is to design and build something robust enough in the first place, so that adaptation is easier in the long term. Don't bother fixing lots of little shelves to suit small objects, build bigger shelves that allow double depth storage of smaller items, you can always add or remove smaller sub-shelves as your need changes.

Shelf construction need not consist of heavy planks, which are both expensive and require large trees. Using heavy timber sections is not an efficient use of timber. If you look how steel structures are built you will notice that solid sections are not used, but 'I', 'H', 'C' and box sections are used which are just as strong as solid sections and are of course less likely to sag under their own weight. Alternatively, instead of using a 300x25mm timber section, it is possible to use three 70 x25mm sections, with a gap between. This can increase flexibility, especially if you need shelves of different depths over the length of a wall. Ideally, permanent shelves should be made out of a timber box section, using plywood and small rectangular sections to minimise weight, maximise strength and minimise cost and waste. The principles that set out ideal shelf construction are well understood in engineering terms, but if you are not an engineer then the following rule of thumb is useful: For the heaviest normally shelf-supported loads (e.g. large books and vinyl LPs), on a 300mm deep shelf constructed to be 25-30mm thick (solid or box-construction), spans should not exceed 2m. That is quite a lot, and you will see from the pictures of the shelf just above the sofa the shelf does actually sag 50mm in the middle on a 2m span (the shelf itself is actually only 200mm deep). This is not in itself unsafe, but it would be better if there was a support in the centre. So in a nutshell, heavy 300mm deep shelves should be supported every metre.

A deep shelf affords the opportunity to support objects in a number of different ways. Large coffee-table books or records can be supported easily, while smaller quarto, A5 or paperback books can be stored in double depth. Equally, it is possible to store small books at the back and have self-supporting objects or pictures in front of them (see illustrations). Or a heavy shelf can be used to support boxes that are accessed as though they were drawers. The important thing to remember is to provide a variety of storage types, and to maintain flexibility of support for changing needs.

Having said that heavy shelves should not be supported off a wall, it is possible to use some very adaptable steel shelving systems that use vertical perforated steel brackets. These modular systems (like the classic Vitsoe 606 system – designed by Dieter Rams in the 1960s) were designed to be fixed to a *strong* wall using multiple fixings up the pressed steel section. These were not designed for heavy loads, or for deep shelving (though industrial versions are available) and they do depend on a strong wall to take heavy loads (and are pretty expensive!). It is possible to use these systems on less substantial walls (e.g. constructed of lightweight plasterboard on timber framing) by first fixing a 50 x 50mm timber section on the outside of the wall first. Ensure that this timber is resting on the floor (i.e. cut a relief for the skirting at the bottom) and if possible jammed under the ceiling at the top. Then fix your pressed section to the timber; this will then ensure that most of the load will be taken to the floor.

If you have a high ceiling it might be worth looking at installing sliding (or rolling) library steps and fitting shelves above normal ground-floor reach. You need to be fairly fit to use these ladders for accessing anything larger than medium sized books, so don't be tempted to display your anvil collection on the top shelf! It is also important that the floor is clear around the bottom of the shelves to allow the bottom ladder track to be fitted.

CUPBOARDS

Cupboards are storage with doors. They can be fixed, built-in or separate storage, even made mobile with the fixing of wheels. Cupboards are used for storing private stuff, Deep Store stuff or stuff that needs protection from dust or prying eyes. Cupboard doors are ideal places for pictures, decoration or can be glazed to allow display of the objects inside.

A cupboard could equally be a set of shelves that has a curtain drawn across it, or perhaps a decorative woven or embroidered hanging. You could use a roller blind, or hinged oil painting.

Internally, cupboards can be arranged in a number of ways. They are ideally used for hanging clothes and odd-shaped objects. If you want a hanging space, measure the length of your biggest coat and set the height of your rail to suit. Though cupboards are generally 500-600mm deep if you do not have enough room it is always possible to slant your hanging clothes to suit. The rest of the cupboard should have shelves fitted. Indeed, in our main room the shelves within the cupboards are contiguous with the external shelves, so the cupboard becomes the main support structure.

If you decide to have a separate cupboard as a piece of furniture (like a wardrobe for fur coats that has a secret entrance into Narnia) then seriously consider fitting wheels

DVD cabinet. Double sided shelving on full-extension slides.

or castors to the base. The bottoms of some economy furniture are not strong enough for this and may need reinforcement so that they can be wheeled about. The main benefit of making your furniture mobile is that you can more easily modify the layout of a multi-functional room without damaging your back. Do not be tempted to use small 'discreet' ball castors, as they are not designed for regular use; instead use swivelling wheels with a 40mm minimum diameter wheel to better spread the load and so reduce the possibility of instability and rucking on uneven carpet.

DRAWERS

Go into your kitchen and pull out a drawer. Measure how far it comes out, and also the internal extent of the drawer. Then measure the depth of your work surface. Chances are that if you have a 600mm deep work surface, the drawer will extend about 300mm, and you will only have about 375mm of internal storage volume. Overall you will have around 200mm or 30% of wasted volume. Replacing those drawers with ones with the same depth as the work surface will recover that space, but until you change the runners to full-extension telescopic slides you will not be able access the entire volume. However, even if you do the sensible thing and fit

World's favourite toy is sorted into workshop drawers.

600mm deep drawers you are unlikely to want to pull it all the way out everyday. For that reason you should divide the drawer in two, put all the everyday things in front, and the back-up tea towels, poultry shears and best cutlery at the back.

Drawers are the kind of storage you need to be able to see into. For that reason, try not to fix everyday access drawers higher than chest-high. Also fix the drawers on removable full-extension slides so that you can take them down for a major organisation, or for cleaning. You will need deep drawers low down for paper files, medium ones for everyday items and shallow ones for particular collections (like photographic collections). If you have a particular place where you work on a hobby (sewing, drawing, model-making etc.) it is definitely worth planning to fit drawers to support your hobby as close as possible to your folding or slide-out hobby work table. It is pretty easy to put dividers in a drawer to separate out your tools or components. Also think about a place to put your work in progress. You could equally design your work table to be constructed from a pair of mobile drawers with a board between.

MOBILE BOXES OR CASES

The key to any successful multi-function space is the mobility and accessibility of the different elements. Fixing a set of braked swivel-mounted wheels to the bottom of a heavy piece of furniture can dramatically transform its utility. At boarding school (the charitable foundation of Christ's Hospital) my trunk was transported to school via train (a British Rail van collected it from our house). It was full of name-tagged sports clothes, books and tuck (biscuits and cakes mostly). The school van collected it at the school station and delivered it to the house, ready for me to drag it into my study. I travel a lot more lightly now! The trunk was a leftover from a journey my parents took across the Atlantic in a Cunarder when I was a toddler. By the time I got to use it for school it smelled of moth balls, as would all my rugby kit and cricket whites (annoyingly – as I am allergic to moth balls).

Guitar bracket with 5 instruments (double-neck acoustic, Les Paul Junior, ¾ acoustic behind, Mexican Vihuela, Hawaian Ukulele).

Trunk-sized packing cases are ideal for holding all kinds of different shaped objects that you do not have to get at everyday. You can fill them with lift-out shallow trays like layers, or divide the trunk into compartments for different kinds of objects. Fix swivelling wheels to the bottom and you can pull them out from under shelves or less-accessible corners. Some trunks were designed to stand with their hinges vertical and so could be opened and used like wardrobes; they would be ideal for storing out-of-season clothes. If you are in a musical group you will find mobile cases invaluable for moving around amplifiers, lights and scale models of Stonehenge.

At school, trunks were often covered with blankets and cushions to be used as seating. Don't bother spending money on an expensive sofa when you can have a mobile storage sofa. Ensure that when you fix wheels or castors to the underside of an item of storage that the castor or wheel is up to the loads, that it is not so small that it is difficult to move or damages the floor surfaces. If your mobile case is lightly built then reinforce the inside corner of the case with a square of 12mm plywood.

HANGING ON WALLS

We are all used to hanging our coats on hooks in the entrance hall, but equally it is possible to hang everyday-use objects on

More instruments behind the door.

hooks behind doors, or even on doors. In our house, apart from some pictures, calendars and the main notice board, we have a number of guitars hanging off the wall behind a door. There is no great trick to this; make sure that the hooks are robust and firmly fixed, either into a timber batten or, if into plasterboard, use umbrella bolts or specialist plasterboard screws that spread the load. Items to be supported on hooks should be fitted with substantial D-rings, heavy loops, or have rope tied securely to them to ensure the item has no chance of falling when the door is opened. All our guitars are stored in padded bags or cases.

The internal doors in our house are of a lightweight hollow construction. This makes it difficult to fix into them to support any but the smallest of hooks. Instead, we have fashioned a simple hook from 0.5mm thick, 10mm wide stainless steel strip that clips over the top of the door. If you make a number of them (they can be made in a small vice or hammered over a wooden former), make at least two for every door, as you will find them very useful for all kinds of occasional uses (such as for Advent calendars!).

If your walls are of very light construction and you wish to fix something heavy to one of them from a single point, you will need to spread the load. This is best achieved using a spreader plate. Depending on the load a typical spread load will be a 300x300mm 12mm plywood square fixed in the corners and in the centre (five umbrella bolts) with the support hook just above the centre wall fixing. If you can, fix into a vertical batten (with a 50mm wood screw). As battens are at typically 600mm fixing centres, a spreader plate has a better chance of taking the load to the ground, whereas a single fixing might tear out of the plasterboard.

HANGING FROM CEILINGS

What goes up must come down, as the old saying goes, and that is never more true than when using a ceiling to support something heavy. It is

Double-pivoting bracket at each end of the two model railways suspended from the ceiling.

inadvisable to hang anything very heavy from a ceiling (e.g. grand pianos, anvils etc.), as a classic cartoon moment will be always waiting to happen. I have seen installations where the bed disappears James Bond-like into a recess in the ceiling, using motor pulleys, a high (>3m) headroom and serious ceiling joists. However, unless you live in a grand Victorian bedsit with 3m ceilings, are prepared to tie your bed position to the set out of the ceiling joists above, and you are patient (and strong), it

is unlikely that raising your bed on synchronised pulleys will be a practical space-saving solution. Instead it would be better, if you have high ceilings, to build your bed on support columns, and climb a ladder to your mezzanine sleeping platform every night (don't forget to fit a fence, or netting to the open side of the bed).

Ceilings, however, are excellent places to store long unwieldy objects such as fishing rods, longbows (we have a 2.4m Japanese Yumi), oars, bicycles, canoes or small model railways. Many of these things can be accommodated using screw-eyes (and expanding plugs) and string loops. For our model railways (see picture) we made nested hinged brackets that allow the railways to come down one at a time. We originally used pulleys but could never get it high enough. Anyone who tries using pulleys will know that you cannot lift anything higher than the centreline of the lowest pulley wheel; any attempt to do so will result in the load on the rope rapidly increasing to infinity as it becomes horizontal.

If you have very high ceilings then pulleys are the safest method of getting your stuff up and down (you can even get small motor winches that have brakes on them). If your ceilings are around the typical modern 2.4m then you may need to use a small stepladder to store or retrieve. In any case ensure that you only move small lightweight items (e.g. fishing rods) on your own. For anything larger (e.g. model railways or cartoon grand pianos) ask for help. It is always worth discussing a safe procedure with everyone before designing the installation, and if you live in a shared house it might be worth having a written procedure displayed next to the item.

STACKABLE BOXES

The ubiquitous stackable box is used for everything. When empty they stack into each other, or can be flat-packed, when full they can be stacked six or seven high. In a compact house they can generally be used in two ways: on shelves, or self-stacked. When on shelves they are used like deep drawers for everyday items. Drawers should not be generally used for everyday items if they are higher than a person's chest (so you can see down into them), however, boxes on shelves can be accessed higher if they can be handled safely (i.e. not too heavy, not too high). We have found them ideal for everyday clothes and toys.

Self-stacked boxes should generally only be used for Deep Store items, as it is necessary to remove higher boxes to get at those further down the stack. Think carefully when planning this; put all the heavier boxes at the bottom for safety when handling, and also mark the contents clearly on a label on the outside of the box, so it is easy to identify where items are and so reduce needless handling. Deep Store items in self-stacked boxes are ideal for storing in low-traffic dead corners. If your stack is really high (>1.5m) then fix a screw-eye into the wall either side of the

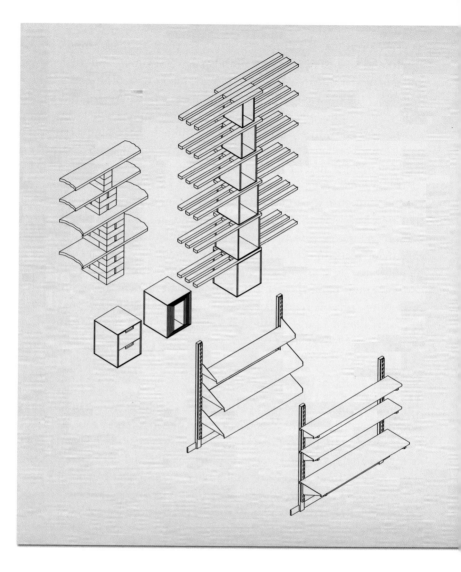

stack two-thirds the way up and string a bungee (hooked elasticated cord available in different lengths) or rope across to stabilise the stack.

If you are very handy it is possible to design your corner box storage to open and close like a Swiss Army penknife. There are a number of ways of doing this: one way is to make a shovel-shaped tray out of plywood just bigger than the storage box. A number of these can then be hinged on to a vertical batten of 25x50mm timber, which in turn is fixed

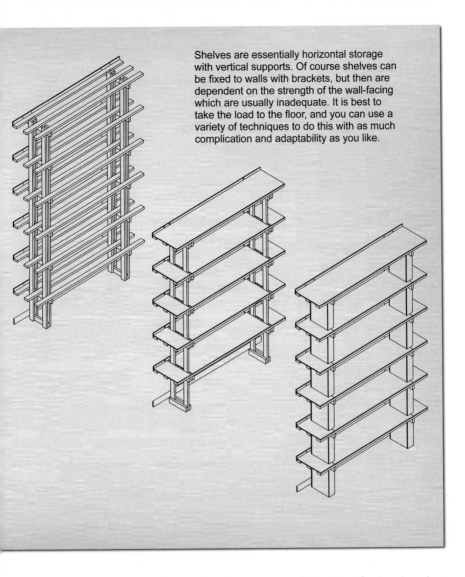

Shelves are essentially horizontal storage with vertical supports. Of course shelves can be fixed to walls with brackets, but then are dependent on the strength of the wall-facing which are usually inadequate. It is best to take the load to the floor, and you can use a variety of techniques to do this with as much complication and adaptability as you like.

to a wall. Accessing a box is simply a matter of pivoting the box bracket just enough that the box can be withdrawn (see picture). If you have access to sheet metal fabrication then something more elegant can be fabricated using welded tubes. Such a method of low-access box storage could be used in conjunction with a cabinet that slides sideways just enough to allow a box to be accessed.

ANY VARIATION OR COMBINATION ON THE ABOVE

Anyone who has been to a reference library will have seen so-called 'rolling storage'. While not really designed for compact living, the modus operandi can be copied for other kinds of storage or display. For instance, we have fitted a section of 25x25mm steel angle to the top bookshelf and use it to hang pictures. The pictures can slide left or right to allow access to the books behind (see picture on page 29). Also, we have combined the design of a drawer with a sliding cupboard to make storage for our DVDs (see picture on page 32). The principle is straightforward, but was a bit tricky to execute using hand tools (I had endless problems sawing a long straight line with a hand saw). I used four 300mm long full-extension telescopic slides to support each cabinet section and a couple of wheels to support the extended weight. The slides are fixed to wooden blocks top and bottom, with the top blocks fixed to the shelf above, the bottom ones to the floor. The only thing I would do differently next time would be to hire a circular saw table to make the cutting easier! In life, the only people that do not make mistakes are people who do not make anything!

Some people have problems convincing themselves on how strong the construction of storage should be. Generally though we grow up with different kinds of storage and have an intuitive sense on what sensible construction is. However, it seems that some people who design self-assembly furniture forget basic principles. In commercial product design there is a consideration for how much something costs to make, and what basic quality is acceptable to the market. *Caveat emptor* (buyer beware)! There is little, if any (though it has improved) self-assembly furniture that is capable of taking much of a load. They are designed to be easy to assemble, cheap to produce, and look attractive when complete. Rarely will you be asked to glue and screw any joints, and as much is made of a chipboard core with a plastic laminate exterior (which cannot be bonded with wood adhesive), and so the joints will be far weaker than the main material. Quite often loads will be taken in cantilever (like a diving board) thus putting more stress on the joints.

It is far better to design the storage yourself. If you do not have the confidence yourself, ask someone you trust to do it. My advice is to have a go on an easy project first, perhaps a simple deep shelf. Think about how the loads are to be transmitted to the ground. Our earliest deep shelves were lengths of 150x25mm timber (doubled to make 300mm deep shelf) supported on columns of house bricks or stout wooden boxes built from plywood (the boxes were ideal for screwing to walls for stability). A support was placed approximately every metre and so would easily take the heaviest loads of vinyl records or books. We then used the shelves for storing plastic crates with odd shaped items, or fitted drawers on telescopic slides. Eventually we organised ourselves and produced drawings of the storage arrangements for each room (see drawings on pages 38 and 39). From the drawings we produced cutting lists. Fortunately we were able to reuse nearly all of the timber from the previous shelving (the trick to that is to try and use the longest continuous lengths possible; it reduces cutting and waste).

Having things slide out, pivot or move around is the key to making storage and spaces adaptable. There is no single method of storage that is ideal from the outset; your storage needs will evolve as your range of stuff evolves. Certain technologies will have an impact on your storage requirements. It may be that in the future the printed book will become less and less prominent in our living spaces, certainly my vinyl collection seems a little anachronistic now. If you have plans to accommodate a particular item in the future (piano, big TV, etc.) then make sure that your design can accommodate with a minimum of fuss. You cannot be prepared for everything life throws at you, but if your storage is sorted then it should be a lot easier (except if you live in a flood-prone area – which of course means that you have all your irreplaceables stored upstairs!).

RENTED ACCOMMODATION

There is always the issue of what to do if you are in rented accommodation (or student halls). It depends on your particular arrangement and contract. Typically there will be clauses that preclude any change to fixtures, fittings or decoration. This will generally mean that you will not be allowed to screw anything to walls, floors or ceilings. While this is a drawback in terms of storage stability it is not an enormous problem. It is quite possible to design storage that is based on shelves between two cupboards. If, along a 3m wall you were to place a 600mm deep, 600mm wide cupboard at each end of the wall it is perfectly possible to fix 300mm deep shelves between them, and use a pair of plywood box columns between them to stabilise them. At the top of each cupboard and top self it is just a matter of making custom sized boxes that are 10mm short of reaching the ceiling and then use timber wedges at the top to ensure the storage is stable (see picture). It is just a matter of dismantling the units when you move out. Obviously the longer the rental period the greater the impetus to sort out something semi-permanent.

Living in furnished rooms, especially on short lets, you are unlikely to live with very much stuff. In fact, it is important that you discipline yourself to living very lightly. However, if you are a mobile contractor, living away from home for months at a time it is worth investigating wheeled crates or lightweight tool chests that allow you to organise your important objects, and perhaps fit a shelf or two between them. It's not much fun living out of suitcase for weeks or months at a time, and in some instances it might be worth renting equipment or furniture locally rather than going to the hassle of buying, selling or carting it around.

ECONOMY OF SPACE IN THE LOUNGE HALL

© Heath Robinson & K.R.G. Browne

42

CHAPTER 6 Folding Beds that Work Every Day

There is nothing more than wonderful than a good night's sleep, and nothing more frustrating than a poor one. Many years' experience of folding beds has brought me to the conclusion that few of them are worth a damn. Often sold as space-saving or for occasional use they tend to suffer from one or more of the following:

- Over-complex mechanism that requires the (too-soft) mattress to be folded many times
- Saggy linked springing that results in back ache and poor support
- Over-soft cheap foam mattresses that lose shape after a short while
- A compromised design that functions poorly as either a sofa or a bed.

The most comfortable bed I have ever slept in was at boarding school. I shared a dormitory with 23 other fellows, and we slept on horsehair mattresses supported on wooden boards (which were sometimes rearranged by the same fellows for amusement). The horsehair mattresses, when new, seemed to provide ideal support, while the daily chore of stripping the bed and arching the mattress seem to keep them in good condition. Years on, my wife and I sleep on a similar mattress: a futon.

In compact living it is almost inevitable that your bed will have to double-up as a sofa. After twenty years we are well used to the discipline of stripping the bed in the morning and folding the bed into a sofa. It takes two minutes and constitutes some gentle exercise. In the West this is an unusual case, in fact most people seems to think that it is beneath them to live like that; which is strange, considering that in very civilised places like Japan this is common sense. Most Japanese sleep on futons that are taken from cupboards in the evening with the bedclothes, and then rolled up again in the morning. It is only in the profligate West that the single-purpose bedroom is so important. It is considered normal to pay mortgage interest on a room that is used primarily for sleeping (or for avoiding the rest of the family!).

It is also interesting how little attention people pay to the comfort of the bed, instead wondering how it will look in a room, with such and such colour scheme. Perhaps the colour scheme is important if you can't sleep because the bed is so uncomfortable and you end up staring at the ceiling. For good sleep you will need good support and a mattress that allows air to your skin. Unless you (or your child) is incontinent do not put a waterproof cover on your mattress, it just makes you sweat, gives you bad dreams and voids the reason for having a bed in the first place; i.e. to get a good night's sleep.

There are a number of different kinds of mattress to choose from, some of which are generally unsuitable for compact living.

INTERNALLY SPRUNG MATTRESS

As they are so inflexible they are generally not considered suitable for compact living, unless stored in a cupboard (which makes a large area of wall space unsuitable for storage) or lifted on pulleys up to the ceiling (unsuitable for rooms with less than 2.5m high ceilings)

FOAM MATTRESSES

Though generally more flexible than other types of mattresses, some are more flexible than others. Generally good quality latex foam mattresses provide the best support, and are amongst the best anti-allergen mattresses you can get (get Talalay process natural latex if you can). However the more supportive the mattress, the less flexible it is, which means that if you want to fold the bed frame you will need to segment the latex mattress. Don't bother with cheap synthetic foam. A bed using a latex mattress can be folded if the mattress is cut into sections at the

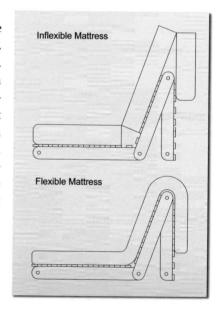

Inflexible Mattress

Flexible Mattress

fold points (see illustration), each section enclosed in its own cover.

Boys bedroom with beds deployed. On a railway couchette the load is taken back to the wall using a complex mechanism. Here, simple removable posts are used.

Boys bedroom with beds away. The bedclothes are bagged and used as cushions.

There is a folding homework desk hinged to the underside of the bottom bed. It is held in place with hinged triangular flaps.

Folding foam cushions can be used as spare mattresses for friends or used as seats for reading or watching movies.

Self-supporting student bedroom assembly (i.e. not fixed to wall). Built of straight-cut plywood and small-section timber this multi-use storage can turn into a large worktable (computer is behind the blind) and bed (the desk is hinged from the underside of the bed). Note split desk provides wrist support for keyboard and mouse.

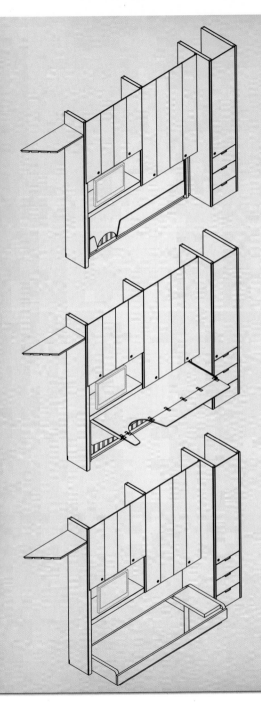

Isometric drawing of the assembly opposite. It always pays to draw something before you build it, it allows you to develop cutting plans, count the number of screws, and it is always easier to change a drawing than modify something once it's been built.

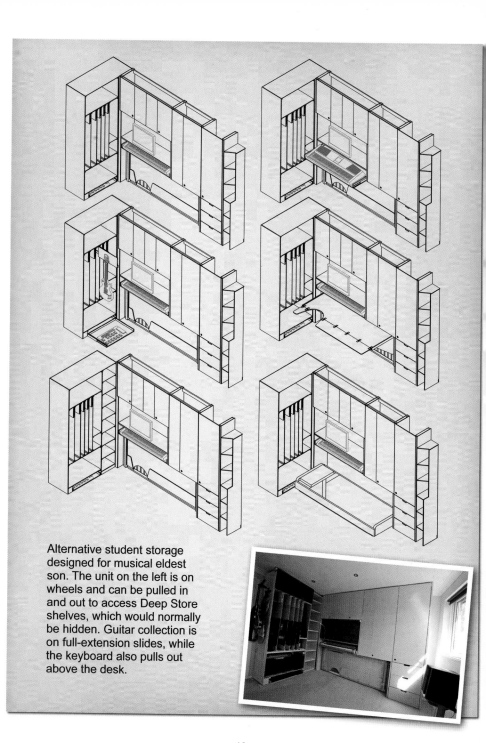

Alternative student storage designed for musical eldest son. The unit on the left is on wheels and can be pulled in and out to access Deep Store shelves, which would normally be hidden. Guitar collection is on full-extension slides, while the keyboard also pulls out above the desk.

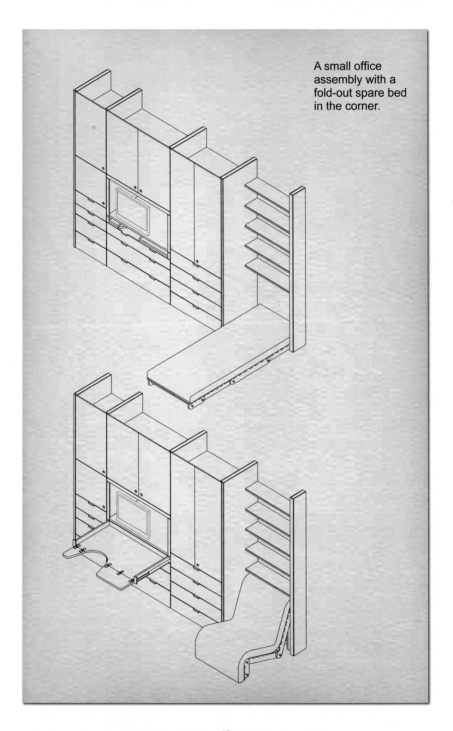

A small office
assembly with a
fold-out spare bed
in the corner.

FUTONS

These are usually stuffed with fluffed cotton (essentially almost raw cotton) or wool and have been used in Asia for centuries. A modern futon is described by how many layers it has (usually six or twelve) and is designed to be used on either the floor or a slatted wooden base. If used on the floor it should be rolled up everyday so that the bottom is aired (if not, mould may appear). We actually use three futons on top of each other. This provides additional comfort when used as a sofa (as a single futon would go hard and flat very quickly). The futons are vacuumed and turned weekly, and re-ordered from top to bottom bi-monthly. On a hot summer day the futons are thoroughly dried on the sofa frame to reduce moisture that could result in mould. However, after about eight to ten years use the futons can be opened and composted – which is not something that can be done with a foam mattress!

In procuring or designing a folding bed ensure it is comfortable, durable, maintainable and easy to change from sofa to bed (and vice versa). After looking carefully at the market we decided that it would be better if we designed and built our own base to suit our purpose and space. The resulting design (see illustration) was pretty simple and has served us well for nearly twenty years. That is not to say that it is perfect; in retrospect there are some changes I would make, to ensure it is easier to convert, change the geometry and lift it slightly to enable it to store the bedclothes underneath. It takes two to four minutes each morning and evening to change its form, but most of that time is taken with the bedclothes storage.

The beds in the boys' room are folding couchettes (see illustration) robustly made of wood with latex foam mattresses. The beds are a tray with slats (for ventilation rather than springing), and M16 bolts are used for pivoting into the 200x50mm vertical timbers. On a railway couchette there is usually a steel mechanism inside the vertical members that provide a spring-loaded balance and a stay for supporting the bed. I could have designed a similar mechanism and had it produced, but it would have been far more expensive and frankly unnecessary as the vertical load is more effectively taken to the ground via the removable posts, rather than via a mechanism to the wall (which in our house are not designed to take that much cantilever).

On the base of the bottom bed I have fitted a folding desk that is used for homework. It had to be quite slim (20mm thick) as when the beds are deployed the desk sits underneath. It took a morning to sort out and was built from leftovers from other projects.

Whatever you decide about a sofa bed (design, materials, construction, and operation) make sure that it fits easily into how your multi-function room works. If you have to move the sofa-bed to get out a drum kit then put both drums and bed on wheels, and ensure to fit some kind of lock on the frame so that you don't accidently deploy it when trying to move it. Our bed-frame is really light, however with the three futons on it we have to flip them one by one before the frame will lift easily. You could, of course, devise some kind of mechanical lift system, using cams and springs, but to do so could bring with it greater opportunities for mechanical failure. Do not forget the acronym 'KISS' – Keep It Simple Stupid, especially if your prototype has to work first time.

An important consideration when considering a good night's sleep is good ventilation. Without at least one air change per hour you are likely to sleep too deeply (due to oxygen starvation) and have really disturbing dreams. In our house we have a small cross-draught across each sleeping room, from a small open back window to the kitchen window (even in freezing weather we have to keep at least a couple of small windows open when occupied as the house is pretty much sealed up when they are all closed). We live in a quiet cul-de-sac and double-glazed (actually we live 50m from the East Coast main railway line, but unlike road traffic it doesn't produce a continuous drone, so we generally don't hear the trains at night). If you do live in a noisy neighbourhood then simple ventilation will be difficult, and it may be necessary to introduce fresh air by means of filtered mechanical ventilation system (the kind with pipes, filters and enclosed fans). A better system is one with a heat exchanger, where outgoing stale air heats incoming fresh air. Such a system is quite expensive and, if you have a complicated room layout, can lead to extensive routing of 150 or 200mm air ducts everywhere.

Sleep is important, as it is part of our natural cycle. Without good sleep we cannot function well for long, and poor health can result from disturbed sleep cycles. In a compact house, sleep is but one of many things we do in our multi-function rooms, but of all the things we design a room for, sleep is the most important.

Talgo kitchen: A modern Spanish Train Hotel kitchen that provides 3 or 4 course dinners for 2 sittings in the 30-seat restaurant car, along with refreshments and hot platters for the bar bistro. It also serves numerous breakfasts in the morning.

CHAPTER 7 | Maximising Kitchen Volumes

Our 3.4 x 2.1m kitchen performs a number of important functions, including that of prep and cooking, kitchen equipment storage, crockery and cutlery storage, food storage, small workshop, occasional office space and laundry. It is fairly typical and as yet is only slightly modified from its original layout. We do, however, have plans to improve its layout and efficiency.

I have had over twenty different employment experiences since leaving school, several in eating establishments (though not as yet in a franchised fast-food restaurant). Each kitchen was different, and each had its own character and way of working. The smallest kitchens were 3.5 x 2.5m corridor type, with three cooks. The largest was around 6 x 6m with additional cold rooms, walk-in freezers and separate washing stations. They were all pretty much constructed of stainless steel (though the Mexican restaurant kitchen used a lot of ceramic tile). There were very few fixed built-in units as it is necessary to be able to pull out every unit in order to clean behind - it is the first place the health inspectors would look. I can still remember the late night cleaning routine of washing the pots, pans, utensils, plates and cutlery, followed by washing the overhead filters, then pulling out the prep units to wash behind, cleaning down all the open shelves. Finally the floor was thoroughly swept and mopped, working from the restaurant access to the changing rooms. If I was lucky I didn't have to come in early to prep for the morning shift.

Professional kitchens differ from domestic kitchens in terms of the materials used and the way they are operated. Professional kitchens are focussed on getting the daily fresh ingredients from the back door, prepped and cooked to the restaurant in the most efficient manner possible, with the minimum of waste. In good kitchens there is always a stock pot or three simmering away, filled with all the leftover prepped vegetables, fish carcasses, roasted bones, etc. Waste is separated between cooked and uncooked, grease residue, and packaging materials are separated into different categories: paper, cardboard and plastic. Everyone in the kitchen works in a highly disciplined manner, with a strict hierarchy

Wagons Lits kitchen: A 1920's kitchen in a restored Wagons Lits restaurant car. With the adjacent pantry, these kitchens were capable of serving over a hundred multi-course covers a day on luxury trains such as the Train Bleu and the Orient Express.

Glacier Express Kitchen: The Glacier Express is a narrow-gauge train that runs between St Moritz and Zermatt in Switzerland. This kitchen is capable of serving 50+ 3-course meals in a couple of hours from an extensive menu. No corner is left unutilised.

determining responsibilities and wage rates. It is very hard work.

Consider then the amazing skill and dexterity of those cooks who work on the railways of the world. On the classic Orient Express of the 1920s and '30s a couple of cooks (and a boy) would be able to produce three to five courses for 60-80 people, three times a day from a tiny kitchen approximately 3 x 2m in area (see picture). There would be an additional separate cold pantry, and an area occupied by the waiters for storing refreshments etc., but the main prep and cooking was in that tiny, hot, bumpy space. The trick, of course was in the menu, which was restricted to items that could be cooked quickly and that did not require huge amounts of complicated prep.

We have eaten in a good number of railway dining cars and are always surprised by the speed and quality of the food. Of course, equipment such as microwaves, steam ovens and salamanders (very hot grills) have helped, but watching the cooks work in those narrow kitchens, I am always astonished by their efficiency of movement.

So how does this affect the design of a compact kitchen? Most domestic kitchens have to service more functions than a professional kitchen. As a domestic kitchen's primary function is food preparation, however, there are lessons that can be learnt. Any treatise, book or magazine article on kitchen design will focus on the work triangle of cooker, sink and prep area. The prep area should be close to refrigerator and the larder (if you are lucky enough to have one). This design focus does tend to telescope a kitchen into quite a small operating area, which is fine if only one person is allowed to work in the kitchen, but too confining if two are working together. In a professional kitchen the prep area is around a metre from the cooker to allow someone to prep while someone else cooks. Also in a pro kitchen there is a separate sink for prepping to that used for washing up. In a shared house the kitchen area can be a social and operational nightmare, unless meals are shared and there is a definite rota for cooking and washing up.

The materials used in the typical construction of domestic kitchens are not designed for either a long hard life or efficient cleaning. Chipboard covered in plastic, vinyl covered worktops, and lots of inaccessible dead spaces and built-in construction mean that internal cleaning and maintenance are compromised. Drawers that are not full depth (see page 32) also mean that you are being short-changed with respect to storage. A typical storage cupboard is also difficult to use as it isn't always easy to see all the contents, and if it is over-stuffed then it is all too easy for things to fall out.

There is much that can be learned from a professional kitchen, but in focussing only on food preparation you could miss opportunities to use your kitchen volume for other tasks. A compact domestic kitchen will have to serve as laundry and larder as well as storage for cooking and eating utensils. Off-the-shelf domestic kitchen units are usually poorly designed in terms of maximising storage, robustness and utility. They are built to serve as part practical and part decorative, without serving either well. Usually built of inexpensive chipboard laminates that dissolve and rot when exposed to high humidity or standing water, they are unsuitable for intensively used kitchens. Better to build in corrosive-resistant metal (aluminium or stainless steel), solid hardwood or tiled

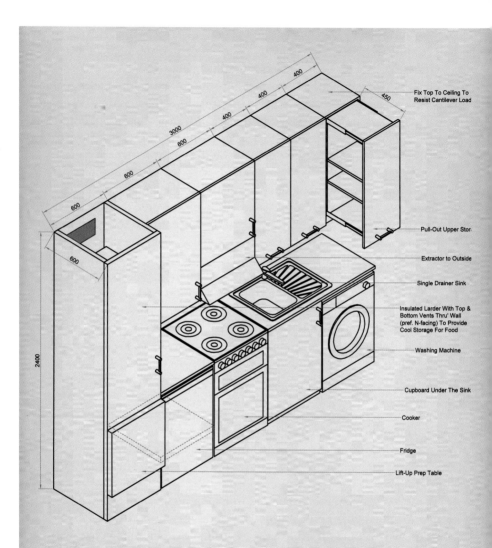

Fix Top To Ceiling To Resist Cantilever Load

Pull-Out Upper Stor

Extractor to Outside

Single Drainer Sink

Insulated Larder With Top & Bottom Vents Thru' Wall (pref. N-facing) To Provide Cool Storage For Food

Washing Machine

Cupboard Under The Sink

Cooker

Fridge

Lift-Up Prep Table

Some much smaller kitchens have been produced, for studio living for instance, but this design is for a fully functional family kitchen. Food prep, which usually takes the greatest space, could take place on a folding table, rather than a work-surface, reducing the number of units. A cool insulated larder, reduces the need for a larger fridge, and provides better conditions for the storage of preserved foods, such as cheese.

masonry. Masonry has the major disadvantage of being immovable and due to constructional section sizes (i.e. the size of bricks) offers relatively little storage, however it is extremely durable and immune to hot utensils (unlike the average vinyl laminate!). All your white goods should be on wheels to ease cleaning behind. Fridges and freezers become significantly less efficient if their heat exchangers (a network of pipes usually on the back) become clogged with dust and grease, so being able to clean behind once a year will save you money.

Like most folk we use our kitchen as a laundry. During wet or cold weather we dry our clothes above the storage heater in the kitchen. This works pretty well, allowing us to dry a load of washing overnight. The downside is that we need to remember to take the clothes down if we are cooking anything aromatic; the children have had to go to school wearing clean white shirts smelling of bacon!

If you have the opportunity to renovate your kitchen before you move in then you can really take some time to think through how everything works and to review the arrangement of equipment within the space. There has been much debate on the nature of dishwashers. Once the machine has been built (with the commensurate investment in manufacturing energy and materials) they use around the same amount energy and water to run as manual washing up. However, the manufacturing resources are not trivial, in addition to the noxious chemicals required to operate the machine, and the enormous quantity of salt required to soften the water. All of the effluent is flushed (out of sight, out of mind) into the sewer to be expensively cleaned. At least if you wash-up manually using a benign eco-liquid it is possible to put the dirty washing up water around your fruit trees. Also, if you are living compactly, like us, you won't have room for a dishwasher, so you can use the space for something more useful.

First, think about the basics: where to place the sink, the cooker, the fridge and the prep area. If you are unable to move the plumbing, gas feed or main electrical supplies then the cooker and the fridge will not be able to move far from their current positions. Next think of the size and specification of the sink, cooker and fridge. If you live alone and tend not to cater for large numbers of people then you will not need a large fridge, sink or cooker. Fridge size really depends on how often you shop, how much you grow for yourself and how often you eat out. If you shop little and often and need only a small volume of chilled storage then you can probably get away with a small fridge that fits under a worktop. If, like us, you have a family and you grow food then you have to deal with seasonal gluts and teenager diet volumes. We tend to shop little and often, as we pass local shops on the way to and from school. We have a double height fridge-freezer (rated A+) but that isn't enough volume for everything, so shopping little and often is the best way of reducing the chilled storage requirement and eating more seasonally.

THE LARDER

Before the advent of mass-produced fridges and freezers it was normal to build houses with a larder. Normally a brick or stone constructed cool cupboard (north-facing if possible) built either just inside or just outside of the kitchen, it had grilled vents that would allow cool air to enter at night and when the vents were closed during the day would maintain a temperature that would allow fresh vegetables, dairy produce and cured meats to keep for weeks. Traditionally, the heavily built larder would have slate shelves to increase the mass and hence reduce the loss of coolness. Often, in warmer months, unglazed jars would be placed in front of the lower grill and filled with water. The water would evaporate, cooling the incoming air. A fine mesh is fitted across the vents to prevent rodent or insect intrusion.

Larders are so effective, that even during the months of June to August it is possible to maintain 4-6°C in a well-placed heavily constructed example. In a freezing winter, the connecting door to the kitchen can be opened to stop the larder from freezing. Unfortunately, nearly all property built from around 1930 onwards was not provided with a larder, and so we have become dependent on electrical refrigeration.

CHAPTER 8 | Even Smaller Bathrooms

If you are moving into a vacant apartment or flat that requires some renovation, and you have the time and resources to make some modifications, then it is a good idea to have a hard look at the bathroom. A bathroom is a high humidity environment, so is unsuited to the storage of books, clothes or other organic absorbent materials (however, that has not stopped some people from over-flowing their libraries into their alternative reading rooms!). If your toilet is separate from your shower or bathroom (i.e. has a separate entrance and ventilation) then finding space for a few books is not a bad idea.

If you are able to review the size of your bathroom and need more volume for storage or living space then investigate whether it is possible to move walls, without modifying the plumbing too much. There are other important advantages to re-designing the bathroom. If you are on

A fairly standard domestic bathroom fitted with a very low-flush toilet, low-flow water fittings and additional bedclothes storage under the window.

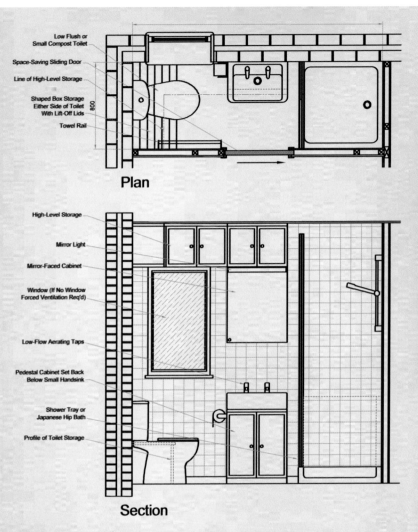

Plan

Low Flush or
Small Compost Toilet

Space-Saving Sliding Door

Line of High-Level Storage

Shaped Box Storage
Either Side of Toilet
With Lift-Off Lids

Towel Rail

800

High-Level Storage

Mirror Light

Mirror-Faced Cabinet

Window (If No Window
Forced Ventilation Req'd)

Low-Flow Aerating Taps

Pedestal Cabinet Set Back
Below Small Handsink

Shower Tray or
Japanese Hip Bath

Profile of Toilet Storage

Section

Above: A compact in-line shower room with toilet. A compost toilet could be substituted for the low-flush, and a Japanese style hip-bath could be substituted for the standard shower tray.

Opposite: The top view shows a square arrangement where a Japanese wet room is separated from the toilet and sink. Japanese washing takes place on the stool using a bucket of soap and water and a handheld shower for rinsing. The compact hip bath is used for therapeutic soaking only.

The bottom view shows a variation on the compact toilet shower-room to be found on some overnight trains. On trains it is generally constructed as a plastic moulding, but here domestic constructional methods are employed.

60

a water meter then continuing to use consumptive fittings will mean that you will continue to pour good money down the drain. You will have to weigh the benefits of reducing the size of your bathroom against the costs of doing so. However, if you are in the process of renovating the bathroom and renewing the fittings then take advantage of low (or no)-flush toilets, low-flow showers, and reduced volume baths and sinks. If at a later date you have the opportunity of changing from a mains

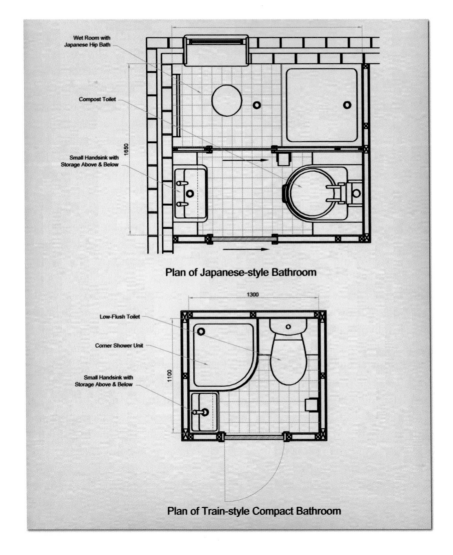

Plan of Japanese-style Bathroom

Plan of Train-style Compact Bathroom

water supply to a rainwater capture system then you will thank yourself for installing lower-demand fittings. In addition, you would have taken the opportunity to convert some bathroom dead-space into living space.

Unless you have to accommodate a wheelchair user, it is possible to design a very compact toilet, based on the spaces found in railway cars. However, it is as well to design for wheelchair use (or easy adaption for), just in case you have a friend or relative that needs that kind of accommodation. Look at the illustrations for ideas.

If plumbing issues (or expense) preclude a drastic renovation then it is possible to use some of your bathroom volume for storage. It may be worth your while separating the toilet from bath or shower, as the humidity in a toilet room will be far less than that occupied by a hot shower or bath. The toilet room can then be used for storing almost anything, though linen is usual. Be advised however, that a damp toilet room can be the ideal breeding place for all kinds of moulds and bacteria, so look carefully at the ventilation, while keeping all stored linen, etc. in closed storage, and not left out open to contamination. If possible, fit a no-flush dry (composting) toilet, and so avoid the possibility of bacterial growth due to anaerobic digestion (composting toilets use aerobic digestion). Composting toilets are ideal if you have room underneath the toilet to fit the chamber, however, most modern houses need significant alteration to accommodate them. It is possible to procure a waterless toilet that has a small batch-composting chamber just under the seat, and uses an electric heater to desiccate the material. Unfortunately for us our toilet is in the north west corner of a house with a concrete pad foundation. This would have made it prohibitively expensive to dig a chamber underneath the structural corner of the house, and our bathroom was not wide enough to accommodate an internal heated chamber. Instead we installed the lowest-flush toilet we could find; this has a 2.6 litre small flush, and a 4 litre flush for 'emergencies'. The toilet has a very efficient low-volume bowl, and with the high pressure flush we hardly need to use the 4 litre flush at all. Most standard toilets use between 6-13 litres of water (sometimes as much as 17 litres) and given that most toilets flush with mains drinking water it seems an extraordinary waste of a precious resource.

Deciding on whether to do without a bath or not is less straight-forward. We are a family of five, and for eighteen years we did without a shower. The reason was plumbing: as our immersion heater is only just above the top of the bath there was insufficient pressure to operate a shower, so we used to share a bath. We renovated the bathroom in 2009 so that we could use low-water-use fittings (the old sink and toilet had developed cracks after being used for twenty-five years), and we changed the bath mixer to one with a shower diverter. We also fitted a hot water pump. We then discovered that five people using the shower in succession (for two to three minutes each) used more water than if we had shared a normal bath. It was only when we fitted a special low-flow shower head that water use was reduced to just under a bath full. Of course, if your household is less than ours then you will save water if you have short showers rather than a bath. Some very low-flow showers are available that give you only ten to fifteen seconds flow at the press of a button, but they do not work with demand-pumped systems.

Baths can perform other functions in a busy household; they are extremely useful for washing large items, such as tents, sleeping bags, duvets etc. If your bathing area is separated from your toilet you could look at having a Japanese-style wet room. A small, deep square bath is used to soak in after washing while sitting on a stool with a bucket of warm water, soap and a sponge (and sometimes a shower). Most baths are large enough for two people, while some come with an internal water heater; many people can share the same water as it is not used for washing. More for therapy than for keeping clean!

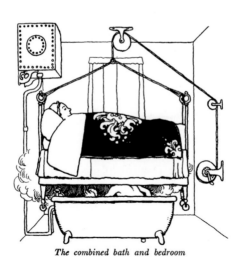

The combined bath and bedroom

© Heath Robinson & K.R.G. Browne

CHAPTER 9 | Sharing Space and Stuff

If you do not live alone, then sharing is the best way of living compactly. With less storage required per person, and the possibility (certainly within families) of passing on clothes or books, sharing also makes for a caring and generally more happy space. Sharing means a good deal of acquiescence, patience and fair deals. It is a place of rotas, duties and timetables; but it is also a space in which many hands make light work.

SHARING SPACE

The issue of private space is one that is often raised when discussing sharing a compact space. Many of us experience extreme compactness on public transport during the great commute. We bear it stoically because we know that it is for only a few minutes, and besides, it's like hitting your head against brick wall, - there is that exquisite relief when it's over! Many of us make private space during those sardine moments with a personal stereo or absorbing book, and we also realise, subconsciously, that what could be a threatening scenario is not because we are all trying to make it seem normal. Social conditioning enables the Tokyo metro to work during the morning and evening peak; so much so that some staff are employed to compress passengers into crowded trains during the rush hour.

Trundling through life we are often faced with transitional periods where there is a shared compact imperative. My first experience of this was leaving home aged 10 to go to boarding school. I had a brilliant time, partly because I was in a well defined hierarchy (social conditioning again) and spent all my time with my peers. We slept twenty four to a dormitory on comfortable horsehair mattresses and wood slat bedframes. The bathrooms were shared, the meals were shared and we did everything together twenty four hours a day. After a year or two the holidays at home felt like staying temporarily in a hotel. It wasn't until I was married years later that I felt at home again. The boarding school experience was, I felt, a good one for me (it did not suit everyone).

Coming from an incomplete home it provided the stability I lacked, and built up my self confidence and discipline.

In order for it to work there needs to be either an enlightened despot, or a strong inclusive democracy. In either case there are rules to be agreed and followed. There has to be open respect for the other members of the household, and a certain amount of gracious acquiescence. The type of household also determines the kind of working system. In a family with young children, the enlightened despot system seems to work best, where the parents are equal and enlightened. With teenage children the situation becomes more fluid and greater democracy is introduced with the understanding that with greater freedoms come greater responsibilities. The certainty is that the situation will always be changing as children get older and their parents mature with them. It would be difficult in a household where there is no meaningful discussion, so it is important that everyone is prepared to listen, and that there is a regular forum for discussion (like a shared meal at the end of the day). In peer-shared households the situation is more complex, as it may start as being democratic but become unbalanced as personalities muddy the rules. The same issues of respect and self-discipline should be understood. I remember all too well my last stint in university halls of residence. Being one of the oldest it was clear that many of the others on the corridor were just experiencing their first days away from their mothers, and I ended up doing most of their washing up for a year; - anything for a quiet life! Whether your living space is large or small it is important that in shared households all the occupants exercises a little self-discipline, and that headphones are an ideal means of maintaining the peace.

If you have the opportunity to design a shared household space, before occupation, then you will have the opportunity to look at the interfaces between spaces. In a shared student or young professional household the bedrooms are separate, and the kitchen, bathrooms and living room are shared. In those situations you cannot do better than having enclosed storage (cupboards with shelves, etc.) lining both sides of any shared walls, especially if they are of lightweight construction.

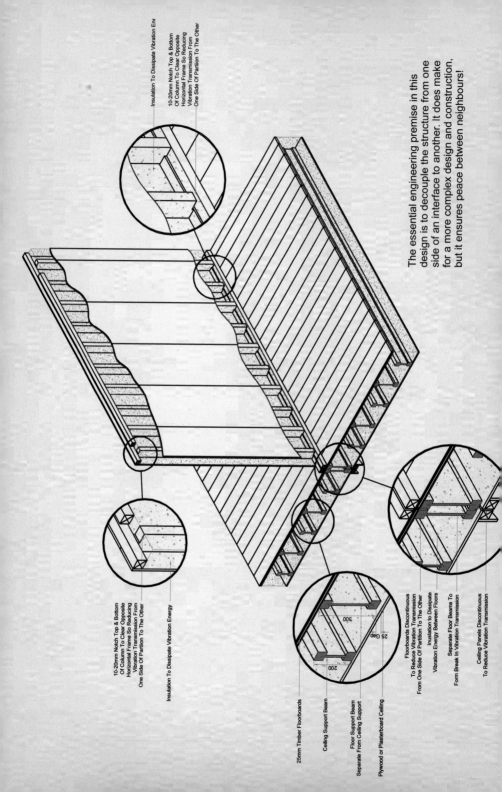

Insulation To Dissipate Vibration En...

10-20mm Notch Top & Bottom Of Column To Clear Opposite Horizontal Frame So Reducing Vibration Transmission From One Side Of Partition To The Other

The essential engineering premise in this design is to decouple the structure from one side of an interface to another. It does make for a more complex design and construction, but it ensures peace between neighbours!

10-20mm Notch Top & Bottom Of Column To Clear Opposite Horizontal Frame So Reducing Vibration Transmission From One Side Of Partition To The Other

Insulation To Dissipate Vibration Energy

Floorboards Discontinuous To Reduce Vibration Transmission From One Side Of Partition To The Other

Insulation to Dissipate Vibration Energy Between Floors

Separate Floor Beams To Form Break In Vibration Transmission

Ceiling Panels Discontinuous To Reduce Vibration Transmission

25mm Timber Floorboards

Ceiling Support Beam

Floor Support Beam Separate From Ceiling Support

Plywood or Plasterboard Ceiling

200

300

25 Gap

SOUND TRANSMISSION

Bass frequencies do not respect walls; transmitting themselves along floors. 20Hz is at the lower end of audible frequencies and has a half wavelength of 8.25m, which means that a room has to be at least 8.25m wide to enclose such a low frequency, and also means that you would have to be more than 16.5m away before there is any appreciable attenuation. Remember also, that even though you will have difficulty 'hearing' below 20Hz, you will feel frequencies down to 1-2Hz (used in some cinemas to replicate earthquakes) which are possible with some audio sub-woofers, but is also emitted by some suburban traffic (and large wind turbines) and is a major contributor to poor sleep. Obviously, in a shared household, low-frequency emissions should be controlled if peace is to be maintained. If you are retrofitting or building, a shared house or flats, then apart from all the insulation, solar panels, rainwater storage and dry toilets also look at interior (and exterior) sound insulation.

The lack of noise abatement is one of the major social problems facing our denser urban spaces. While studying at Brunel in west London I could never get used to the incessant jet noise coming from Heathrow. A plane would fly low over my building every ninety seconds from very early in the morning to late at night. In an age before Mp3 players I would often find myself reaching for the headphones attached to my record player, just to keep myself from flinching when the next plane came over, while trying to write an essay or produce a drawing for an assignment. It was very difficult to maintain a train of thought, or get a good night's sleep; I often wonder if the constant noise in our cities is not a major contributor to mental illness, or do we just get used to it?

The disadvantages of everyone wearing headphones is that we stop engaging socially (though it can be difficult to hold a conversation while planes, trucks and cars are going past, or on public transport), and we are less aware of our surroundings. In a shared household it is necessary to fit a smoke detector and fire alarm in every living space, however it is equally important that the fire alarm also activates a bright light, with a flashing component, so that someone wearing headphones (or could be hearing-impaired) is alerted in the event of an emergency. It might also be useful to have a flashing light connected to the door bell, just in case you can't hear the knock at the door.

The transmission of sound can be significantly reduced through simple design changes. If you know where your dividing walls are going to be then it is possible to discontinue the floor boards at the division so that foot falls on one side of the wall cannot be felt on the other side. However, there will be some transmission due to shared floor beams. Unless your room divisions align from the bottom to the top of the house with solid load-bearing construction there will always be sufficient transverse sound transmission requiring some understanding between occupants. One lightweight party wall construction detail (see adjacent detail) is to decouple the two wall skins (plasterboard or timber) by building an out-of-phase doubled sub-frame so that the skins do not share the same vertical posts. You will need to insulate between so that any vibration in one skin is not transmitted to the other one. Of course, doubling the thickness of plasterboard increases the mass of the wall and significantly lowers the resonant frequency of the wall (making it better at absorbing lower frequencies).

Unless you decouple floors above from ceilings below, foot fall transmission will also be an issue. It is pretty straightforward to cure when retrofitting a building, but difficult to retrofit when occupied. The essence of a good design resolution is not to fix a ceiling to the same beams for the floor above (see adjacent detail). Also look at door construction; poorly sealed lightweight doors are not good at isolating corridor conversations from adjacent rooms. If you can change the doors to a heavier construction (fitting 30min fire-rated doors may be legally required in any case) and fit a pair of seals (intumescent for a fire seal, foam seal for sound insulation). A better solution is a pair of doors, one opening outward, the other inward. In any case it is worth fitting a door bell (and light – just in case the occupant likes listening to headphones) to each private door.

A particular problem to some shared buildings is the effect of music practice. Our youngest is learning alto sax and due to the nature of the saxophone it is very difficult to attenuate, unlike a brass instrument, as the sound from woodwind instrument emanates through the valve holes as well as the horn. Believe me we've tried everything; electric saxophones do exist (very expensive), but they tend to have different fingering and breathing techniques, and so are not a useful alternative. At least with a trumpet it is possible to use a mute as all the sound is produced at the horn. The eldest plays electric guitar and bass which are ideal as they can be played quietly acoustically or through headphones, similarly with the electric piano; while the middle boy can practise drums either on a rubber pad or an electronic drum pad which uses sensors under the skin and transmits it to an amplifier (and so can be practised with headphones). Acoustic instruments, such as percussion, stringed instruments (violin, cello, acoustic bass, acoustic guitar), acoustic pianos, etc. all have reasonable electric equivalents which can be used within a sound-sensitive household, though they do not behave exactly the same.

LIFE'S TRANSITIONS

Living alone for long periods is contrary to the social needs of most humans, and yet it is sometimes in the most densely populated places on Earth that loneliness can be a serious mental health issue. Leaving home under any circumstances can be a distressing time. And while leaving is part of life's journey for most people, the transition for many can be traumatic. In my case it was gradual, as I became used to living most of my life away from my mother from an early age, time at home always felt temporary and transitional. Transition from school to university was almost seamless, and then to living in London in a shared house while working, also felt temporary. It was only when I married that I felt at home again. Now my children are facing a similar future of secondary school to university; the house will transition from being full to becoming empty. How will they deal with the new, with the loneliness, the insecurity? Life is a journey; wisdom is only gained through experience; knowledge only really comes with learning from mistakes. Becoming a parent has been a joyous though sometimes painful experience. I feel blessed by it, though it is a responsibility that is sometimes too great to bear. You try to think of everything, and yet my dreams are still full of the terrors of losing my children through accident or malice. As a parent you invest your whole being into the future happiness of your children, and yet you took it for granted as a child that your parents would always keep you safe. Sharing a small house as a family with teenage children is probably the hardest thing anyone has to do (outside of deep deprivation or living in a warzone). A teenage brain goes through enormous changes in just a few years, and along with the dramatic hormonal changes it is no wonder that teenage and parent do not often share the same sense of reality. The teenage years seem to be spent trying to understand an alien world while struggling with profound insecurities and endless homework. This living in alternate realities but in the same space can be trying, all the more so as both parent and child are both feeling their way through this for the first time. For that reason all parties need to communicate honestly and freely with each other so that respect is maintained.

SHARING STUFF

In a family home the issue of stuff-sharing is far less important than in a peer-shared household. In student houses (especially where students are new to living away from home), it can sometimes be difficult for some folk to understand the difference between sharing and borrowing (or recognising that mould on a pizza might be related to its inedibility!). The rules that dictate responsibilities or shared tasks should equally refer to particular items (usually food or equipment) and these should be respected as individually owned and off-limits.

In a family household it may be useful to introduce children to the idea of the responsibilities of private property quite early, though at the same time reinforce the idea that Sharing Is A Good Thing. Different households and characters may have a different idea, but I think it is important that respect and responsibility are instilled at an early age.

A convenient little morning room for breakfast

© Heath Robinson & K.R.G. Browne

CHAPTER 10 | Designing for Health and Durability

As an asthmatic I have a morbid fear of houses with Victorian-style clutter; nowhere to put a mug of tea, every surface covered in dust-collecting trinkets. In a compact house there are several aspects of storage design, space layout and materials that will have a bearing on how much maintenance will be needed, the build-up and control of moisture, dust and mould, and hence the durability and health of your compact space. It is important that if you invest your time and money into your living space it does not make unnecessary work or affect your health. You need to be able to access easily behind all your storage, especially if it is against any external walls. During the winter, depending on the construction of your external walls, it is possible that moisture from breathing and cooking will condense on the inside, resulting in lifted paint, wallpaper or plaster. Microbes in the air (such as fungal spores or bacteria present everywhere in the atmosphere) will use the damp walls on which to propagate, resulting in further significant concentrations in spores or exudations that can affect your immune system. Some can also digest your wall finishes, and eat into timber framing, so affecting the structure of your building (rising damp). As the concentration of activity in a compact space is greater you need to pay particular attention to how your space is finished and maintained.

OVER-EXTENDED FINANCES

The property ladder mentality can often lead to financial risk-taking and desperate debt problems, and can also lead to poor mental health that will further undermine financial liquidity. It's a nasty little spiral. The relationship between property prices and wages is so extreme that most people struggle to make payments even when interest rates are low; when interest rates double, say from 1% to 2%, interest payments will double, forcing many people to make very difficult decisions.

Of course the main premise of this book is for people to accept (and thrive) living in smaller places; doing this will expose you to less financial risk, potential pain and stress. It is extremely unfortunate that many people, having stretched their finances to afford a house, then do not have enough to carry through basic maintenance. Their house starts falling down around their ears (for want of a nail), and then they are in a worse situation as their property devalues and they cannot afford to move.

In permaculture we suggest that when undertaking a large project, you assign only a third of your resources to initial purchase, and hold on to the other two-thirds to develop and maintain the site. This is a conservative approach to property development that has demonstrated its value time and again. By not sinking all your savings into initial purchases, your reach will never exceed your grasp. Instead of unfulfilled dreams, you will enjoy a realised comfortable state of compact bliss. Many people are likely to give you advice, many of whom will pass on the standard advice of getting one's feet on the property ladder and to try and expand your horizons to larger and larger property (whether you need it or not). A larger house will not make you happier, and an over-extended house will increase your liabilities and maintenance worries. Just think how much you would save in the long term not building that extension and instead vouchsafing the garden for growing food, plus using the money to ensure that your house is in good order, well insulated, efficiently heated and lighted and perhaps generating your own power and saving your own rainwater. It may seem normal to aspire to a luxury five bedroom executive mansion, but it won't make you happy if you have to work yourself to death to afford it. Instead aspire to happiness by not stressing yourself.

DUST AND TRAFFIC

People make dust as they interact with their environment; it is the natural outcome of everyday wear and tear. The more durable the surface the less dust is made. Living compactly means that high-traffic areas are likely to receive more wear than in a similar usage expansive house (though in general the bigger the house, the more cleaning there is). Dust and fluff will collect in low-traffic areas as it is blown around by the traffic. It will collect in corners, under furniture, on furniture and in carpets. If allowed to become moist through humidity or damp it will provide a substrate for mould, mites and other insects (e.g. silverfish and carpet bugs). A compact space can be cleaned more quickly than a larger space, but it has to be done more often as there will be a higher concentration of dirt; all part of the discipline of compact living.

If you do have the opportunity to choose materials and finishes for your compact dwelling it is always better to go for natural materials, though avoid using woven fibres or grasses for any high traffic areas as their durability is not high. In my late teens we were living in a rented furnished house, as the builders were still making my mother's new cottage habitable. My mother found some attractive woven grass matting in the garage of the house and put them in the kitchen in the run up to Christmas. My asthma worsened greatly during the next week and on Christmas Day (and my 18th birthday) I was in Pembury Hospital being relieved with Adrenalin, unable to breathe. Needless to say the grass mats did not re-appear. If you suffer with allergies be wary of any woven materials, as in a compact house the air volume is reduced and so allergen concentrations will be significantly higher. This is especially noticeable when buying in furniture or using paints that are treated with volatile chemicals (especially formaldehyde). That is the primary reason for constructing nearly all the furniture in the house myself and only use water-based emulsion paints. However, when we go away on holiday (locking all the windows) the house seems to acquire a particular smell; the same from when the house was first built 30+ years ago. The smell seems to come from the walls and is characteristic of chemical off-gassing, so be warned. Needless to say we open all the windows when we return.

We have found by experience what finishes do not survive in a compact household: cork tiles, softwood floors, cheap rubber-backed carpet and cheap vinyl tiles (at least for hallways – though they have survived in the bathroom and kitchen). Materials that do stand up to traffic include: ceramic tiles (not porcelain), hardwood flooring (depending on the coating), bare concrete (if it is sealed, otherwise it is very dusty) and heavy-duty

In high traffic areas soft materials, like cork tiles, wear too quickly to be cost effective.

carpet. If you have hard floors it is always possible to put rugs down to make it softer under-foot, though remember to not use rugs in high traffic hallways as they will decompose fairly rapidly if exposed to muddy feet. If possible try and store outdoor shoes near the front door to reduce the ingress of outside matter all around the house. In Japanese houses the entrance way is generally below the level of internal rooms. There is a place in the entrance or lobby where outside shoes are stored and where indoor slippers are exchanged when entering the house. In a compact space a small amount of dirt goes a long way so it makes sense to avoid it arriving in the first place.

In any house dust will accumulate in areas where it becomes trapped or where it migrates from high-traffic to low-traffic zones. Carpet is an ideal place to trap dust, as are bookshelves (and the tops of books). If you have hard floors dust will accumulate behind doors and under sitting areas. Computer equipment is notorious for accumulating dust. Many a laptop in our household has died from over-heating due to dust build-up in the heat exchangers. Computers with removable cases may be less mobile but at least you can vacuum them inside once a week. Controlling dust is a matter of common sense. Putting doors on your bookshelves (glass ones if you can accommodate and afford it) is ideal, but not always practical, otherwise it is a matter running a vacuum nozzle or damp cloth across them whenever the problem becomes noticeable. Try not to use a dry or feather duster as this simply spreads the problem elsewhere, and of course you well end up breathing it in – a real pain if you are asthmatic.

MOISTURE AND FRESH AIR

Modern houses are generally built with some kind of vapour barrier liner just inside the outer (usually brick) skin. The purpose of this liner is to provide a controlled location for the condensing of moisture-laden vapour travelling out through the wall of the house. If water were to condense in the outer skin it could freeze in the mortar, or result in internal damp. Unfortunately, liners are not completely effective as they are quite often damaged during construction, or not well detailed around widows or vents. In conjunction with well-sealed double-glazing the result can be an unhealthy build-up of stale moist air. In a compact household this can happen quite quickly unless steps are taken to avoid it.

For that reason it is important to make sure that all storage built on external walls is open, e.g. shelving. If you build closed storage on an external wall you will risk the build-up of mould behind any units or paper stored there. If you do have shelves on an external wall, fit a small batten at the back of the shelf so that books cannot be pushed all the way to the wall, therefore protecting them from any winter damp.

The most obvious step to avoiding stale air is to open a window. Actually two windows is better, one on each side of the house. Try to get a cross-breeze. Ironically, it is more important to do this in winter (when you least need having cold air rushing through the house), as you will normally be spending more time indoors breathing, cooking, and making hot drinks. You will not need to open the windows very much (in our small flat a couple of windows are kept open 25mm or so all through winter. Of course, if you have a forced air ventilation system (with a heat exchanger that recovers most of the heat from the out-going stale air to heat fresh incoming air) then you should have little trouble. Unfortunately most of our building stock either does not have such a system or is not designed to take one, so we are stuck with opening the windows!

Generally you want to have at least one change of air per hour in any occupied room. If you have a very large room and there is only one person in it then less new air is necessary, but if you are having a very active party in your bedsit then more air exchanges per hour will be required. Of course, opening a window invites increased noise exchange, which might put you at risk of a visit from the noise police, or the distractions of traffic and planes.

HEATING AND COOLING

Ideal house construction would entail the whole external structure being breathable, well insulated and massive enough to provide some heat inertia. Strawbale construction is almost ideal as the tightly-packed straw walls are heavy, well insulated and yet allow vapour to pass through it slowly, giving up any moisture and heat in the wall before exiting. A strawbale wall is coated on both sides with a plaster, softer on the outside so that vapour tends to transmit more easily from inside to outside. Of course the building needs to have large overhanging eaves to stop the walls from wetting easily (wet walls do not transmit vapour easily), and the walls tend to be really thick (300-500mm thick) which reduces potential internal volumes; but overall the performance of a strawbale wall is much better than a typical brick-clad wall for healthy indoor living. And as for the lower internal volumes, with sustainable compact living it's easy!

Keeping a compact living space warm is relatively easy, compared to an expansive space. Less external wall area means that more of the heat you produce in the house (from cooking, washing, laughing, etc) will stay within your living space. A concentration of more people per cubic metre of house will ensure that per unit area of external wall you will more Watts of heat generated. A well insulated external wall will slow down the transfer of heat from the hotter side to the colder side. In winter the heat transfer will be from inside to outside, in high summer it is more likely to be from outside to in.

In our small flat we only have one small storage heater, and even during the cold snap of 2009/2010 we only needed to have it turned up to halfway. We didn't choose to install the storage heater, it came with the house, along with three others that we removed as being unnecessary. The house was built with single-glazed windows that simply poured winter heating from the house; a change to double-glazing made three-quarters of the heating unnecessary. Needless to say our heating bills reduced dramatically, paying back the double-glazing investment in less than five years. However, given the choice, we would have liked to have had under-floor heating installed, which would have brought with it some insulation from the un-insulated cold concrete slab.

In summer the cold concrete floor is a boon, though due to our smaller floor space the benefit is less than in a larger house. Our ground floor situation is cooler than our neighbour upstairs, though when everyone is at home on a hot day it can be difficult to stay cool enough. Ironically, throwing open all the windows can exacerbate the problem as hot air will heat up everything inside of the house, so taking a long time to cool down at night. During a hot summer it is actually better to open all the windows at night (or at least an hour or so before dawn) and then close them during the day, fitting shutters to the outside to stop sun reaching any south-facing windows. Note: drawing the curtains inside the house doesn't help as much as the hot air will be trapped between curtain and window and then convect to within the room. Better yet to fit external shutters with reflective overlapping rotating horizontal blades. By rotating the shutter blades it is then possible to set the angle appropriate to the conditions: on a hot summer afternoon have them set so only a small proportion of light is reflected up onto the ceiling to give internal ambient light; on a bright sunny winter's day reflect the light downwards on to the floor to warm it up, instead of it blinding everyone with low-angle sun.

It is amazing how much you can control the comfort of your living space with carefully placed external awnings, shades and shutters. If you have access to the outside of your house (i.e. you are not living high up in a block of flats without a balcony) then it is possible to control the climate inside your house with judicious planting outside. Ideally you will need an open space on the north and south sides of your house (or north and south balconies for a flat). For a hot summer, grow climbing (edible) plants on the accessible south wall to reduce the sun heating the wall, and keep the shutters closed. On the north side fit a shady awning to maintain shade and surround the back door with shady herbs (like mints) that you will keep watered so that they respire cool, moist, scented air into your living space. In winter shutter the north door, and build a temporary double-glazed sunspace to the outside of your south door. Fill the sunspace with a small lemon tree and herbs. Remember to insulate the sunspace at night to avoid night frost.

In the UK at least, living compactly is often associated with living in squalor. It doesn't have to be. If you think it through, organise yourself and prepare properly there is no reason why living compactly should be any more of a health hazard than living expansively. It certainly takes less time to keep clean!

© Heath Robinson
& K.R.G. Browne

CHAPTER 11

Inside/Outside

One of the main criticisms of living compactly is one of claustrophobia. The fear of enclosed spaces afflicts a good many people, but actually far less than commonly expected. Usually claustrophobia is confused with the sense of a space smaller than we are used to, and as such does not need medical intervention! A properly designed and maintained compact space does not actually feel too small, but there are ways of increasing the feeling of greater space without actually needing to get the builders in. It is a symptom of poor design that tricks people into thinking they need to build an extension, therefore losing garden area. Quite often the result is ill-advised and poorly built, and you are left with a structure that leaks, requires constant maintenance and actually devalues the property. Before considering an extension, ask yourself whether you are using your current space efficiently first.

INSIDE

The tricks to making your space feel larger are as old as the hills, literally. In Japanese garden design there is an ancient technique known as *shakkei* or 'borrowed landscape'. Essentially, a Japanese garden designer arranges the plants, rocks and constructed elements so that from the position of meditation the garden seems as though it is part of the larger, 'borrowed' landscape, such as a distant hill or forest, even though the garden might only occupy a few square metres. For a compact space the trick is to determine where you will be spending the most time (in my case it is by the back window at the computer). That will be your main focus position; another one might be where you sleep, or the kitchen sink (hopefully positioned near a window). Hopefully you have the relative benefit of a large window nearby, and through the window an attractive landscape. My view is our productive back garden, which even in winter, is full of promise. If your view is less than attractive then you can change your focus from far to near. Our kitchen window is usually full of herbs, seedlings and fragrant flowers; we have fixed a glass shelf

Borrowed landscape: In Japanese garden design distant views are often 'borrowed' to augment the garden. The design of external spaces or internal decoration can often used to hide poor vistas or 'borrowing' good ones.

halfway up so that we can double the number of seedlings. If you have a very poor view you could consider fixing a stained glass window (or stick on a vinyl temporary one), however, stained glass will significantly reduce the amount of natural light and change the colour of the light inside the room. Perhaps a small mobile of coloured glass hanging at the window would provide a sufficient hanging distraction away from an unattractive view.

Window size has a huge impact on the feeling of space in a room. Even if your view beyond is less than inspiring, having a larger window gives more opportunities for growing food without reducing internal light levels too much. If you have large French windows out onto a balcony or garden it is worth working out if you could fit an extra set of doors 300-600mm inside (or outside) to make a small greenhouse. The extra glass doors are designed so that the plants are supported on shelves fixed to the door, so when the door is opened the plants move out of the way. A little wheel on the door prevents the hinges taking too much load. Of course both inner and outer doors would have to be fitted with operable vents so that the mini-greenhouse does not overheat; a rather extreme conversion perhaps, but a good idea for new build or eco-renovation.

The best arrangement of windows in a room is to have light coming in from two sides; as the sun moves round during the day the room illumination changes, making it more interesting. If you have only one window then it is worth experimenting with internal reflection. If you cannot see directly out of a window from your main sitting position it may be possible to see a reflected view. A really good way of experimenting

When we first moved in to our compact house we wanted to start growing food almost immediately. We turned the rear patio into a growing space by lifting the pavers and cementing the corners. It worked quite well until it rotted the neighbour's fence!

We started to grow veg by reading the backs of the seed packets of things that looked interesting to eat. 20+ years on we are still learning!

Part of the later garden when we discovered railway sleepers. Here potatoes are grown in recycled car tyres. As the plants grow another tyre is placed on top filled with compost. It uses a lot of compost and needs watering everyday, but produces a lot of potatoes.

with this is to fix some kitchen foil to a large flexible board. You can then trial fitting the foil-board to walls, cupboard doors and ceilings, and in front of book shelves to get a good experience of the effect. Also look at what happens when you curve the foil-board. This will change the width of the view. Once you have settled on a position and size you can either go to a glazier to have a piece of mirror glass cut, or you can obtain a piece of reflective aluminium (usually around 0.5mm thick) and glue it to a piece of hardboard, which in turn can be flexed to achieve the width of view you want. The glass is more hard wearing and easier to clean, but the aluminium will be much lighter (because it is thinner – aluminium actually has a very similar density to glass) and is therefore easier to fix. And of course, reflective aluminium is much harder to break, making it ideal for cupboard doors.

It makes sense to paint a compact room in bright colours to lift it, using white for ceilings, doors and door frames. However, if you spend a good deal of time inside (e.g. working from home) a lot of white or magnolia can be particularly depressing and un-inspiring. Libraries are good places to work in, as almost everywhere there are books, with their variety of spine designs and titles to provide you with inspiration. If you have bland white walls break them up with important pictures that you can see while you are working. As described earlier in the book, you may have important talismanic objects that provide you with comfort. Make sure that they are displayed in a (safe) place that you can glance upon when you need a little encouragement or inspiration.

OUTSIDE

If the human race is to survive beyond the end of the age of oil we will need to grow more food where we live. Key to this is not building large houses on the best quality land. Also key is the fact that the freshest food is the most nutritious, giving home-grown food a vital role in ensuring human sustainability. As resources become depleted and the infrastructure more expensive to maintain due to the inevitable increase in oil prices as it disappears, it becomes necessary to recycle more resources closer to their point of use. Whilst this is covered more fully in the next chapter (Off Grid Possibilities), there is much that compact living can do to better integrate the inside and outside spaces. Fitting slide doors instead of hinged doors can reduce the amount space taken by opening them, though they are

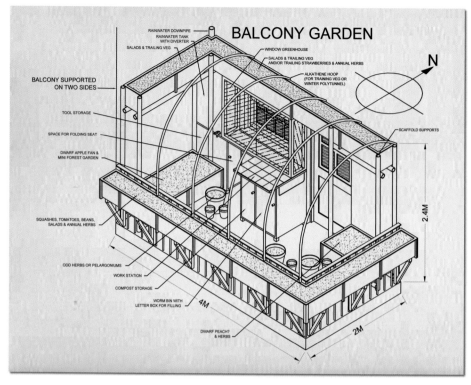

BALCONY GARDEN

RAINWATER DOWNPIPE
RAINWATER TANK WITH DIVERTER
SALADS & TRAILING VEG
WINDOW GREENHOUSE
SALADS & TRAILING VEG AND/OR TRAILING STRAWBERRIES & ANNUAL HERBS
ALKATHENE HOOP (FOR TRAINING VEG OR WINTER POLYTUNNEL)
N
BALCONY SUPPORTED ON TWO SIDES
TOOL STORAGE
SCAFFOLD SUPPORTS
SPACE FOR FOLDING SEAT
DWARF APPLE FAN & MINI FOREST GARDEN
2.4M
SQUASHES, TOMATOES, BEANS, SALADS & ANNUAL HERBS
ODD HERBS OR PELARGONIUMS
WORK STATION
COMPOST STORAGE
WORM BIN WITH LETTER BOX FOR FILLING
4M
DWARF PEACH? & HERBS
2M

usually more expensive for a comparable level of sealing and insulation.

If your house or flat has access to an external space, whether it is a garden or balcony, there will always be possibilities for growing food. There are plenty of books on how to do this (I even wrote one myself!) but if you are really new to gardening the best thing to do is to practise with a few herbs and salads. Obviously there will be a limit to the amount of planting, water barrels or construction you can place on a cantilevered balcony or roof garden. You will need to ensure that all the heavier loads are placed or fixed to load-bearing walls. If in doubt make friends with a structural engineer.

Herbs basically come in two types: annual and perennial. Annual herbs, such as parsley, coriander, basil and chives (there are many more) are generally grown from seed, sowing into small pots of free-draining compost or soil, transferring to a larger pot (potting-on) when the seedlings are fully developed. You can cheat by buying supermarket herb pots and simply potting on to a 150mm diameter pot (the

On top of our compost enclosures we built a mini-greenhouse/hotbox. We lined the inside with aluminium foil to reflect the light around to stop the seedlings becoming too leggy.

The strawberry tower was a way of growing a lot of strawberries in one place and be able to move them around with e sun or to move out of the washing on the line.

supermarkets sell them in 50mm pots so they get root-bound quickly – and they therefore don't last long). Annual herbs can last for months if you keep them watered, but it is worth re-sowing once a month spring to autumn, and then freezing any excess for winter use (though basil is best preserved in olive oil as freezing tends to destroy the taste).

Perennial herbs such as sage, rosemary, thyme and mint are usually grown from cuttings and sold in small pots. All but mint are derived from dry Mediterranean wild plants that thrive in hot climates on poor alkaline soils. Pot your cuttings into 300mm pots filled with gritty compost and water them until you cannot feel any water 50mm below the surface. Mint needs to be grown in water retentive compost and watered often. It is a plant more often found growing in the wild near streams and in shade, so put them in open shade.

All herbs can be grown on a window sill, both inside or outside. A window box can be fitted to the outside window sill, whilst inside a windowsill can be extended inwards with a shelf. In that way taller plants can be grown behind shorter plants just behind the window. If you can, pivot the inner shelf so that you can access the window box without having to move the indoor plants one at a time.

In permaculture design there is the logical premise that elements that need the most looking after should be closest to the centre of occupation; simply put, grow your herbs, salads and soft fruit closest to the back door. In a compact house or flat there is little point in growing large quantities of main-crop fruit and vegetables as you simply won't have the room. Instead it's better to grow leaf salads, tomatoes, chillies, strawberries and perhaps a small apple tree along with the herbs mentioned above. Unless you have a reasonable amount of ground-level soil, don't bother with big root crops (e.g. potatoes, parsnips, large carrots, beet etc.) as some of them need to be grown in feet of soil. Having said that, massive competition carrots and parsnips are often grown in 2m long tubes! Grow leaf salads that re-grow from stems that have been cut before, don't try and grow large head lettuce (like Iceberg) because the supermarket varieties are usually grown hydroponically (i.e. without soil) and need almost constant watering, unlike the leaf types.

If you have a spot with constant warmth and light it might be possible to grow a dwarf lemon or clementine tree. They do require the soil/compost to be changed annually (very carefully!), but they can produce a useful crop and emanate a wonderful blossom scent. Dwarf apples (on M27 rootstock) can also be grown in large (500mm) pots outside. It is better to obtain them as bare-rooted maidens (i.e. in the first year after grafting) in winter. They will take around five years to come into fruit, though it is possible to buy five year old trees from nurseries, but do not transfer them to a new pot until they have dropped all their leaves in winter. You will also need to learn to prune them to keep fruiting and free from disease. Very dwarfing M27 rootstocks slows the growth of the apple tree, but that means that they are not as resistant to fungal diseases or insect attacks.

In summer, your outside space becomes all the more important. Whilst you have to remember not to let your interior space get too hot (see above), the outdoor space becomes an extension of your living space. I know of some people who sleep outside during summer nights, even when rain threatens, by using an awning or bivvy tent. In any case, make sure that you make space for a seat and small table in amongst your plant pots, and under your grapevine.

Living in a compact space is a matter of perspective; if you do not see your space as small then it is less likely to bother you. By ensuring that wherever you are inside you can see outside, the issue of internal space seems less important. Borrow the outside to become part of your inside.

CHAPTER 12 | Off Grid Possibilities

Nearly all of us are dependent on grid utilities; electricity, gas, water and sewerage. We are so dependent that it is considered a threat to life and limb if any one of them fails to function. And yet it was not always so, and does not need to be in the future.

Major utilities require a massive network of pipes or wires to flow or transmit their utility to you (or away from you in the case of sewerage), they also need huge plant to produce and control their utility, along with an army of engineers and office staff to maintain and charge for the utility. They are big corporations, and control much of your life. But does it have to be so? The corporations depend upon you not understanding how to do it for yourself, and yet it is fairly straightforward, providing you are prepared to invest time and money.

WATER AND WASTE

So what does it take? You need water and sewerage utilities so that you can re-hydrate yourself, cook, clean and use the toilet. Water comes from the sky, and for the UK this is not an issue. It is merely a matter of capturing water from a roof, having enough storage enough to cover your needs in dry spells, and a means of filtration and pumping to point of use. It is surprising how little water you actually need on a daily basis if you have the presence of mind to install low-water use fittings and a dry toilet; perhaps as little as ten litres per person per day. Having a dry toilet also means not having to treat sewerage. Instead all that is needed is a means of treating greywater, which can be as simple as a settlement tank and an under-soil perforated pipe under the soft fruit patch (however, there are some effluent and planning issues which will need to be resolved with your local council, so it is worth hiring an expert).

Whilst not easy to achieve within a single flat in a block, it is possible for blocks of flats to be designed that does provide for its own water and water treatment. For a house, shared or family occupied, it is relatively straightforward to invest in a rainwater catchment system. There are many suppliers of components or complete systems – just look on the internet.

ENERGY USE

Home energy generation is already well established. Again, it is a matter of investment in knowledge and money. From the outset you must separate the energy that is used for lighting, cooking and heating (and perhaps cooling). This is because there are steps that should be taken to reduce the requirement for energy before planning any investment.

We take it for granted that we must fit low-energy light bulbs to reduce our carbon footprint. Compact fluorescents and LEDs are exchanged for incandescent bulbs and in so doing can reduce our lighting energy demand by 80%. It is also important to look at where our lighting is and how it is arranged, so that lighting energy is not wasted. Different types of lights are suitable for different tasks. Large work requires a large lit area, either from a number of parallel long fluorescent fittings, a large circular fluorescent some distance a way or from a smaller mobile fitting closer to the work. You have to decide for yourself. You may wish to add ambient lighting for eating or entertainment; this is generally reflected light (off a coloured ceiling or wall) and mobile task lighting can be used for this purpose.

It seems obvious, but during an average day most of your lighting can be provided by the sun. Artists prefer indirect white light in which to paint, so an ideal studio would be an attic with large north-facing windows. Before double-glazing, these studios would be freezing in winter, perhaps resulting in more than one early death from pneumonia amongst the painters of northern Europe. Any window with a view of the sky can provide an ideal working light, with those with a southern aspect providing an interesting variability of illumination through the day, though the possible disbenefit of overheating or excessive glare (which can be controlled with variable angle slatted shades).

Reducing your light energy requirement will save money in the amount of generation you will need to invest in, as well as the cost of maintenance, or the re-purchase of grid electricity should your generation system be grid-connected.

Cooking is another area where a good deal of energy is required. Electricity, gas or solid fuels are typically used. In a compact household electricity is perhaps the easiest to use, however with up to 7.2kW possible on a 30Amp connection, it is quite difficult to deliver that much power for any length of time on a domestic self-generated system. In northern Europe we tend to have a diet that uses extended cooking. A classic extreme comparison would be between Ireland, where slow cooking on a fire laid with the relatively inexpensive (or free) dried peat fires is used to cook relatively tough cheap cuts of meat, and China where ultra-fast high heat cooking is used, both to maintain nutrients and because fuel (often biogas) was far less available. While an extreme example, cooking methods and diet can have a great bearing on the amount of cooking energy needed. Obviously, using insulated slow-cookers, woks and microwave ovens will use only a fraction of the energy of an old oven or hob, but only if you change your diet to suit.

Cooking or heating with natural gas requires an additional connection to your compact house; and whether you use grid or bottled gas means tying yourself to a non-renewable supply. Biogas is an alternative, but due to issues of scale and ambient temperature is not really suitable to colder climates, or to households where a great deal of animal effluent is not available (which is pretty much everyone except farmers who keep a large number of animals indoors). An alternative that may find its way into a domestic setting in the not too distant future is the use of hydrogen.

Most domestic energy generation systems can be split into two types of excess energy management: battery storage or national grid integration. Batteries (usually refurbished deep-cycle submarine batteries) have been the mainstay of off-grid electrical storage for many years, but they are heavy, expensive and require a special storage area. The alternative is to sell excess power to the national grid (using a special meter) at less cost than buying it back. An alternative for the future may be hydrogen storage as an alternative to batteries. Instead of charging batteries it may be more useful to split water into hydrogen and oxygen, storing the hydrogen. The stored, pressurised hydrogen could then be used to generate electricity via a fuel cell or used instead of natural gas in a cooker.

If you are living far off-grid and have access to a sustainable wood supply then it makes technological sense to invest in a solid fuel stove with back boiler to heat water. In a small well insulated house these can actually produce too much heat, and during the summer can be a serious disadvantage unless your kitchen can be made part of the outside of the house (by opening a glazed wall for example). Do not be tempted to lessen your insulation so that you can have your stove on all year round. It is better instead to highly insulate and build a heat-retaining ceramic stove (e.g. Kachelofen) that works on the principle of a short, quick hot burn to heat up the mass in the stove. This dissipates slowly; you'll have to use more conventional means to cook in the hot summer months.

To heat a house, the cheapest, most direct method is to use the sun. Unfortunately it is also the most difficult thing to control. Passive solar heating design is often considered a black art, as it is difficult to balance the level of insolation (solar energy that enters through the window) with mass absorption, insulation, aspect, and control of overheating in summer and excess glare from low-level sunlight in winter. In fact it is so tricky that most people who build conservatories on their houses fail to orientate them properly: Fitting on a south elevation will lead to overheating and condensation within the triple-wall roofing; on a north elevation there will be constant even light from the sky which is good for painting, but precious little heat from the sun except in summer, otherwise it will stay cool; on a west elevation it doesn't warm up until the afternoon, which is less than useful in the summer when you are already too hot.

The author's photovoltaic roof panels. In conjunction with the use of low-power fittings in the house, and the use of the mains supply to balance the load, it is perfectly possible to produce more electricity than is consumed. Note space on left awaiting the installation of water-heating solar tubes.

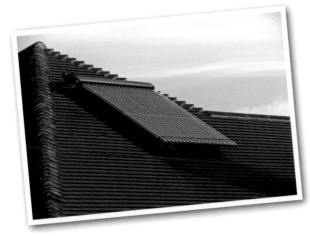

These evacuated tubes are connected to a heat-exchanger within the hot-water cylinder to provide year-round pre-heating of hot water. During the 3 summer months no other energy is need to heat water for baths and showers.

The only sensible place to build a conservatory in northern Europe is on the east or southeast elevation so that it warms up in the morning when you need it. Sunspaces can be built on the side of most structures, even apartment balconies. The essential component of their design is to capture winter sun, but shade out excessive summer sun (unlike a conservatory, which has a glazed roof and lets in sun all year round). They are also ideal for growing out-of-season food. Sunspaces should be used to heat up some mass heat storage. This can be as simple as black barrels full of water, or as complex as a solar hypocaust – underfloor mass storage that moves warmed air around the house.

There are other means of pre-heating incoming air, including a Trombe wall, which is essentially a shallow greenhouse built against a black painted wall. Air vents top and bottom allow air to be drawn from inside, heated behind the glass and then vented inside; cycling continuously during the day. On cold nights the vents are closed and the warmed wall radiates heat collected during the day. The external walls have to be really thick to work well; often thin walls are used which do not store sufficient heat during the night, while the un-insulated external glazing, if not covered at night, will lose much of the heat destined for inside. Trombe walls need to be very carefully detailed to work properly, though the principle has worked better as a greenhouse where human comfort is less of an issue.

Through good design it is possible get most of your heating from the sun. For back-up heating there are a number of options, all of which will have a bearing on the level of technological and knowledge investment. We use a single storage heater in our small flat, mostly because it came with it. Our flat originally came with four, but after fitting double-glazing it soon became apparent that we only need one. Unfortunately our ground floor has cold floors as the slab is not insulated from the ground. This is useful during a hot summer, but in winter we tend to wear three pairs of socks and if we were building from scratch would probably insulate the slab and install underfloor heating (even though the single kitchen storage heater also dries our clothes in winter).

Underfloor heating does have certain advantages and disadvantages. The main advantages are the high comfort level and even heating. Unlike a roaring fire or wall radiators, high radiating temperatures are not needed, and there is less chance of cold spots away from the fire. The main disadvantages of underfloor heating are that to be really efficient, they need to be combined with an insulated heavy floor and cast in with a ceramic tile surface for good heat transfer. There are kits that allow retrofitting, but they tend not to be very durable and significantly increase floor thickness (e.g. you will lose 50-75mm on door and ceiling heights), and if your ceiling height is a standard 2.3-2.4m you will certainly notice the loss of headroom. Due to the relatively low temperature of an underfloor heating system it is particularly suitable for connection to a Ground Source Heat Pump (GSHP) or Air Source Heat Pump (ASHP), that use a refrigeration-type heat that moves energy from either the ground or air into the house. The relatively low temperature of the energy from a heat pump compared to some form of electrical or combustion source means that it is easier to feed an underfloor heater, which only runs at 20°C or so.

ENERGY GENERATION

All renewable energy apart from geothermal and tidal energy is generated by the sun. Wind is a result of air rushing from a high pressure zone to a low pressure zone (air is heated by the sun and increases in pressure), solar energy can be converted into electrical energy directly using photovoltaic panels, or can be used to heat water directly using solar water panels. If you live in Iceland choose geothermal as hot rocks are much closer to the surface there than almost anywhere else on Earth. Otherwise, if you want generate your own power and be less dependent on the national grid, photovoltaic and/or wind generators are generally the power source of choice. Photovoltaic panels have improved their efficiency enormously since they were first developed for electrical generation in space. It is now possible to install photovoltaics with better than 10% efficiency (~100W/m^2), payback times of less than four years and life spans of around twenty-five years. There are plenty of suppliers, and if you have a reasonable area of roof with a southern aspect it is definitely worth investigating.

Typical 5kW horizontal wind turbine: If you have a constant source of wind (e.g. live on a hill) then a wind turbine can provide power when the Sun doesn't shine. This a fairly typical 5kW horizontal axis unit.

Unfortunately the sun doesn't shine all the time, so in the UK there are far more wind turbine installations than photovoltaics. Essentially, a propeller on an alternator (or DC generator), most turbines are horizontal axis devices that pivot on a bearing so that they can rotate to face into the wind (though some are downwind facing in operation). Wind turbines will only work in a range of wind speeds, too fast and they engage a device that brakes or offsets the turbine so that it does not get damaged. Vertical wind turbines are perhaps less efficient but they generally work in a larger range of wind speeds and from any direction, which is ideal in an urban environment where nearby buildings can deflect winds in different directions, depending on wind speed (rotational turbulence from building corners). Payback time on a wind turbine is typically less than photovoltaics, but for domestic installations it is harder to make less conspicuous as you will want to mount your turbine as high as possible to keep it in clean air thereby reducing pulsing due to turbulence. If you want to install a machine larger than 500W it is advisable to get a specialist to do it. In any case, with the installation of either photovoltaics or a wind turbine check if you need planning consent.

Sometimes the sun doesn't shine and the wind doesn't blow (like the January day on which these lines are being written). For those times it will be necessary either to switch everything off or use some kind alternative supply. If you are way off grid then you will have to invest in some kind of energy storage. Local energy storage usually consists of a collection of batteries, sized to suit the nature of your system. Refurbished deep cycle ex-submarine batteries are used out of choice, as car or truck batteries are designed to provide high current for only short periods and are not really suitable for situations where you need a nearly constant current for long periods until the battery is nearly completely discharged.

An alternative method of energy storage currently (at time of writing) being prototyped and researched is the use of fuel cells. Fuel cells in many ways work like batteries, with reactants being catalysed in an electrolyte to separate electrons from protons and drive them in a circuit. Much of the research is trying to remove the need for platinum (an expensive strategic metal used in jewellery, car catalytic converters and industrial processes) as a catalyst, and to improve design to drive costs to around £20/kW.

In essence, when your generation exceeds your usage the excess electricity is used to disassociate water into hydrogen and oxygen. The hydrogen is captured and pumped into a foam-filled pressurised tank (the foam in the tank precludes an explosion if the tank fails). When there is insufficient power to run your household the hydrogen is used to power a fuel cell that converts the hydrogen and atmospheric oxygen back into water and so generating electricity.

Both fuel cells and batteries produce Direct Current electricity and it is possible to fit a house with a range of DC equipment (lights, fridge, TV, etc.) that are designed for use in small boats or caravans; however, most electrical

In urban areas with tall buildings high winds can be a problem for horizontal wind turbines due to the constant change in wind direction. For those situations a vertical axis machine, like this 5kW Eddy GT unit from Urban Green Energy, can effectively generate power.

equipment is designed to be used with Alternating Current. To convert DC into AC you will need an inverter. Inverters are pretty sophisticated now and can be used to control charging cycles and generate computer reports on the health of the system.

The other main alternative supply is the national grid. Many people who generate their own power, instead of investing in batteries, sell their electricity to the national grid. This only requires the use of a special synchronised inverter and meter. Your electricity needs to be in phase with the Alternating Current produced by the national grid and you will be paid at a tariff (much) less than what you pay to buy it back. If you have a very reliable supply (and if your supplier is tied to renewable generation) it can make economic sense to not invest in local (battery) energy storage and instead use your grid energy supplier as storage.

Finally, we use a good deal of energy heating water for washing ourselves, our clothes and for washing up. It is much less efficient to heat water with photovoltaic electricity than it is to heat water directly from the sun using solar water heating panels. There are basically two types: an evacuated tube or flat plate collector. The premise is the same: the sun shines on a black painted surface that is in contact with the water. The water heats up and can be pumped to a heat exchanger in a modified domestic hot water cylinder where it preheats the water. Evacuated tube collectors can operate at much higher temperatures than flat plate collectors so that in some cases (e.g. hot summer) can heat a domestic cylinder to such a high temperature that it does not need further heating before use. Flat plate collectors are generally less expensive, less efficient (especially on cold days), but can be home made using a few plumbing supplies. Apart from your collectors you will need to re-plumb your interior hot water supply to ensure that your solar circuit does not overheat in summer or freeze in winter (evacuated tubes very rarely freeze as they are better insulated from the cold and use an anti-freeze in their working fluid). Generally the extra plumbing revolves around sizing and installing the additional pre-heating cylinder with the heat exchanger inside. You will also need some kind of expansion control device and a cistern to supply your cylinders. You do not need to re-plumb the whole house, but you will need to find room for the extra plumbing around the cylinders.

Living off grid is much easier if the structure has been designed to do so from the outset. Quite often retrofitting an older property will bring with it too many compromises to make it economic. Much depends on solar aspect and how much basic refurbishment is required. If you have a derelict property and have deep pockets then you can afford to rebuild your house with external strawbale insulation, a ground source heat pump and underfloor heating, solar panels for heating water and generating electricity, hydrogen energy storage (and for cooking), and a sunspace for preheating the interior of the house and growing extended-season food. If you live in a flat the opportunities for independently retrofitting off grid equipment is limited. It is only when a whole block is refurbished that it becomes more cost effective, with insulation and the fitting of low energy equipment the most cost-effective action. For a block of flats to go off-grid for water is highly dependent on being able to fit a dry-toilet system, which is not easy given the normal routing of soil pipes. To become energy independent also requires good solar aspect, both for passive solar heating, and for solar panels. Tower blocks are usually pretty well situated for the installation of vertical axis wind turbines given the way they tend to funnel turbulent wind between blocks.

A Pump for Using the Bath Water in the Garden

© Heath Robinson & K.R.G. Browne

Off grid living is especially well suited to those living far from grid services in a purpose-built eco-house. Such a house can be very compact, fitted with all today's modern conveniences, and yet be inexpensive to build and cost almost nothing to run. The trick is to build within your means. If you can build it all yourself, do not deplete your savings and then go nuts. If things are a little tight and you need to pay for expertise or additional muscle, however, start small but make sure your designs allow for any reasonable additions (apple store, chicken house, extra water storage, etc.) when you can afford it. One thing is for sure, we will all need to be ready when energy prices soar.

CHAPTER 13 | The Future, and How It Affects Your Stuff

It is almost impossible to live compactly in isolation. The way we live is often a reaction to the times we live in, the kind of society, the technologies and the resources we have access to. Human epochs have been named for the different technologies or cultures that marked that particular age, whether it be Stone Age, Renaissance or Industrial Revolution (more of an evolution actually). These epochs did not simply start and stop but overlapped and evolved from one to the other. With a little imagination we can imagine that we are probably at the end of the Oil Age, at the beginning of the Information Age, and culturally in the middle of the Celebrity Age! We are definitely not living in the Green Age.

At present our culture almost wholly depends on oil for almost every aspect of human economic activity. Every basic resource, from raw materials to food supply and most of our transport energy, is at risk once the oil supply is compromised. Almost every job, and therefore nearly every culture, is dependent on oil, and yet by 2100 we will have exhausted all the easy to exploit oil reserves. There are reserves of bitumen sands (currently being exploited in Canada), but as this is sticky and heavy it does not flow under its own pressure and requires a good deal of high-pressure steam – which of course requires a significant percentage of the extracted energy to exploit it. This may be just as well, as excessive fossil fuel use has increased carbon dioxide concentrations to levels not seen on Earth for hundreds of millions of years, resulting in unequivocal global warming, ocean acidification and sea level rise. As terrible as it may seem, I often look forward to the end of oil, as it would mean that I could then breathe in our congested cities (40+ years as an asthmatic leaves certain antisocial scars).

So what will the world be like in the run up to no oil? It is easy to speculate, but hard to be accurate. If we try to read current trends and draw a straight line into the future, we can fail to see any forces that might change the direction of the line we've drawn. It looks as though efforts are being made to reduce carbon emissions, but the trend is still up, though it is likely to drop as resources start to dry up. The big developing economies of China and India (and the surrounding states following on their coat-tails) are now consuming more and more as they play catch-up with the West. Unfortunately, these developing countries cannot afford the latest 'clean' technologies and so are building cheaper, and dirtier, and these inefficiencies will accelerate our undoing. They are trying to raise the standard of living in their countries (rightly), but in doing so are exploiting those least able to move with the changes as Western companies move their manufacturing and services to where the labour costs less. The new middle class feeds aspiration, drives up wages, which will make the developing countries less attractive for manufacturing. China and India will not be able to maintain their economic growth for long (perhaps to 2020) before their relative economic parity will stall their programmes, unless they change their direction towards an economy based on sustainable technologies and greater social equity. The West is already facing this dilemma, and it will not go away. We are living on the verge of either social collapse or a new age of sustainability.

Living compactly, efficiently and self-reliantly tends to shift focus away from wasteful technologies and cultures, driving the market towards more sustainable local economics. Today we are living with the result of the actions of a few avaricious bankers, whose culture of high risk has left high unemployment, depressed global economies and increased pressure to re-grow economies and pay off national debts using any means possible; inevitably unsustainably. Governments have a difficult job, and we don't make it easy for them. They have to balance the aspirations of their electorate with their ability to pay for it all. World peace, food for all, good education, healthcare, etc.; the budget battlegrounds are demarcated whilst the media plays with the truths and speculations that sell newspapers and corporate advertising. Or so it used to be.

The invention and development of the internet may provide an additional balancing force. Already it has shown how democratic it can be; culturally it has the potential to be all things to all people. It is inclusive and providing there is sufficient bandwidth does not require a powerful computer to access, and so is becoming more important in the developing world. It is important that the technology can become more sustainable in its manufacturing and maintenance if we are to sustain its democratic purpose.

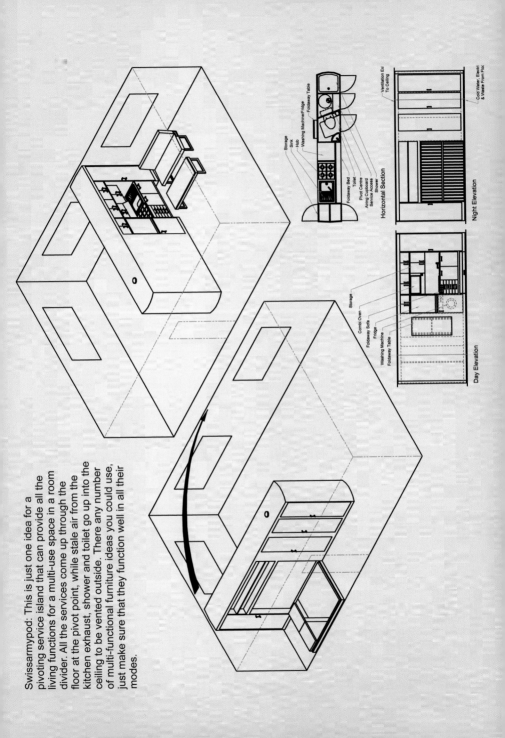

Swissarmypod: This is just one idea for a pivoting service island that can provide all the living functions for a multi-use space in a room divider. All the services come up through the floor at the pivot point, while stale air from the kitchen exhaust, shower and toilet go up into the ceiling to be vented outside. There any number of multi-functional furniture ideas you could use, just make sure that they function well in all their modes.

Storage
Sink
Hob
Foldaway Bed
Toilet
Pivot Centre
Airing Cupboard
Service Access
Shower
Washing Machine/Fridge
Foldaway Table
Ventilation Ext To Ceiling

Horizontal Section

Storage
Combi Oven
Foldaway Sofa
Fridge
Washing Machine
Foldaway Table

Day Elevation

Cold Water, Electri & Waste From Floc

Night Elevation

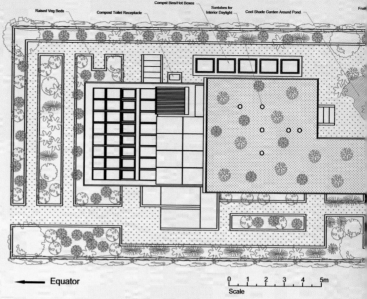

Raised Veg Beds
Compost Toilet Receptacle
Compost Bins/Hot Boxes
Suntubes for Interior Daylight
Cool Shade Garden Around Pond
Fruit

← Equator

0 1 2 3 4 5m
Scale

30m x 12m Suburban Garden Plan with Compact Family Ecohouse

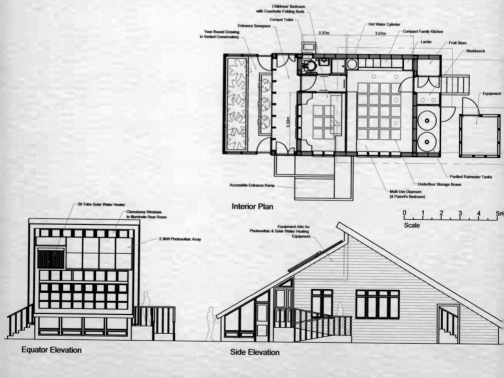

Childrens' Bedroom with Couchette Folding Beds
Compost Toilet
Hot Water Cylinder
Compact Family Kitchen
Entrance Sunspace
Year-Round Growing in Vented Conservatory
2.37m
3.57m
Larder
Fruit Store
Workbench
3.92m
Equipment
Accessible Entrance Ramp
Purified Rainwater Tanks
Underfloor Storage Boxes
Multi-Use Dayroom (& Parent's Bedroom)

Interior Plan

0 1 2 3 4 5m
Scale

20-Tube Solar Water Heater
Clerestorey Windows to Illuminate Rear Room
2.3kW Photovoltaic Array

Equipment Attic for Photovoltaic & Solar Water Heating Equipment

Equator Elevation

Side Elevation

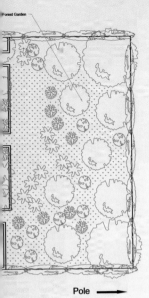

Forest Garden

Pole →

This is a design for a self-reliant family house on a typical 30 x 12m plot to be found in most suburban areas. The living space inside is multifunctional and designed to maximise the production of food in a permaculture garden. It could be constructed of timber, strawbale or earth, depending on local available materials. The roof could be reinforced to support more soil, which would allow the growing of soft fruit and salads (shallow-rooting wildflowers or sedum is more usual on a lightweight green roof). Please note that this design was produced by an engineer, to enable efficient function and construction; architects would have different ideas!

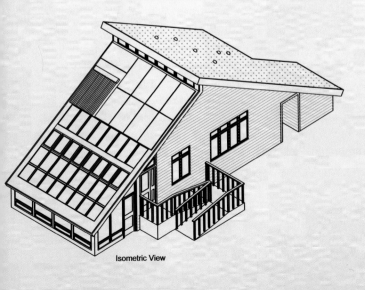

Isometric View

Certainly, information technology is enabling us to live compactly. It's not all good news however, as we will see. The giant move to digital information creation, editing and storage means that entire encyclopaedias can be stored and accessed from a small disc of silvered plastic. Storage densities are increasing all the time, with 1TB (1,000 GB) soon possible on a credit card sized device. But what do we do with this storage? We can store all our books, correspondence, music, videos; in fact almost everything that identifies our lives. And we do not need to store all this information at home. With the increase in broadband speeds it sometimes more convenient to store your information and programmes on a remote computer, a 'cloud', so that you can access and edit it wherever you are in the world, using a relatively inexpensive low-powered device (or even a mobile phone). And because all this information is remote from your computer, if your computer dies (and believe me they do with alarming regularity), your information is safe and can be accessed again once you have either repaired your machine or borrowed another. Unfortunately it is not as simple as that. The Cloud is not free, it is a subscription service, and if you fail to pay you will lose access to your stuff, and perhaps, eventually your stuff will be deleted. Also, being a commercial service, it is subject to market forces and it is always possible that your cloud company could cease trading, with you losing access to your information; which all means that you will have to back-up your stuff at home anyway. It is a discipline that rewards an ordered mind. Losing work or important correspondence (and who hasn't) is deeply frustrating, so even if you decide to save your life on the Cloud, make a back-up at home. I currently save everything to small plug-in hard drives, with a secondary back-up to DVDs. This is a never-ending process; while the DVDs may last twenty years; the hard drives only have a life of five to ten years, so if the data is important you will have to continually invest in new hardware. Digital photographs and video are particularly difficult as ever increasing resolutions push up file sizes and so increase pressure on hardware. You will never need less digital storage.

So how will that impact the future? The internet is dependent on an ever developing network of optical fibre, powered by national grid connections with nodes and servers all around the globe. It all needs maintaining and renewing, and while a stable global civilisation exists there is nothing to worry about. Of course, there is a never ending battle between those who wish to disrupt these virtual democracies and most of us who just want to get on with our lives unmolested: it's just like 'real' life. If we are going to live our lives online then we need to educate ourselves to ensure that we benefit from it and not become unwitting victims. Unfortunately we cannot take anything at face value, so websites have to earn our trust.

In the not too distant future I imagine we will be able to carry around our 'lives' on a wristwatch-sized device, talking or corresponding instantly with people across the world using audio jewellery and sunglasses that are actually high-definition TV screens. Will we notice the world outside anymore? I don't own a mobile phone so I am often bemused by seeing people utterly preoccupied with the little boxes in their hands, restlessly waiting for someone to call them, and when a call is made the conversation seems utterly inane and of little purpose. Perhaps mobile phones remind us how lonely modern life can be. Me? I just read and meditate; and I don't think I'll be changing anytime soon.

As we won't need physical storage for our books, records, movies and pictures we can live all the more compactly. Some designers have been speculating on designs for the ultimate in compact furniture for compact living spaces. Some use the adaptability of the small travelling caravan with its expanding sides and roof, converting kitchens into tables into beds and then disappearing into a cupboard. Such caravans can be built as pods to be installed in blocks or singly. Separate energy/water modules can be plugged in to provide for services. I particularly like the penknife-style furniture 'tool'. All the furniture is housed into a central island about 3m long, 1.2m deep and 2.4m high. The island houses a toilet/shower at one end (the electricity, water and waste connections are aligned with a socket in the floor) and has a kitchen range on one side and all the requisites of a bed-sitting room on the other side. Tables, bench seating and beds all pivot out from the island rather like a penknife, with storage supported on telescopic slides. The whole island can be moved and stored against a wall when not in use, or when the maximum floor space is required; a bit like science-fiction, but interesting. There is any number of multifunctional furniture available that can be compacted into a cube or wheeled case, for instance

If we are to live sustainably we need to live in cohesive communities, rather than in the alienating urban environments that planners have provided for us so far. Community spaces, green corridors and a move away from car dependency and cul-de-sac thinking are all vital if we are going to survive without wanting to kill each other. We need to make our world a garden where all life can thrive. A rather naïve 1960s ideology perhaps, but isn't the purpose of life to find meaning? The world's food supply is not guaranteed, and developing land once used for agriculture reduces the amount of land remaining for growing food. A move to more self-reliant communities that grow and recycle locally brings with it stronger local economic bonds and a more sustainable social structure. If we continue to truck food from everywhere to everywhere, when the oil disappears we will no longer be able to fertilise, spray pesticides and herbicides, or plough the great big fields that agro-industry uses. We will also not be able to package, process or store food in the huge central warehouses that the supermarkets depend on.

The future is always unknown, and the uncertainties bring with it a certain level of fear. The media often prey on us with their dark projections and portents so that they can sell more papers (bad news always sells more than good). We end up believing it and it becomes self-fulfilling, feeding the media with more tales of woe. To keep sane it is better to not buy into it, to think optimistically, logically and do the best you can. Also, probably best not to watch soap operas! While the future may not be all hover cars and household robots, technology will change and we need to be better educated before we become dependent on yet another unsustainable toy.

While all the above may seem to be rather depressing, it is not out of our hands yet. Once you have grasped the idea of low-impact compact living you will find that you have much more time to empower yourself and inspire others. There are some wonderful movements and empowering ideologies such as the Transition Movement and Permaculture that have the power to reign back the consumptive stupidity of this age. These are the key to changing the direction of that straight line to Armageddon, the important balancing force that effectively pits the consciousness of the silent majority against the forces of unsustainability. Even now, good scientists and engineers are finding ways of doing more with less, of building smarter adaptive technologies that can be translated into developing countries without becoming even more dependent on oil, rare earth metals or transportation from the ends of the Earth. There is still a light shining for sustainability, for a rich, interesting and fulfilling life; we just need people to see it by holding it up.

CHAPTER 14 | What To Do Next?

So you have read this small book and are faced with compact living, either by choice or through one of life's twists. What do you do next? Psychologically there may be a tendency to do nothing at all, especially if you are downsizing due to a change in circumstances. There may be an irrational belief that you will win a prize or lottery that will return you to a more expansive situation. While it is always good to be optimistic, it is far better to see this change as liberation, and a chance to live more freely and lightly.

You need to meditate on the positive; you need to think how wonderful it is going to be once you are unsaddled of all that junk! You need to think of new beginnings and new possibilities. Make lists, lots of lists and start sorting. Make sure that you make room for the important things like making tea, hot food, a comfortable place to sleep, somewhere to wash and importantly, some music to make work lighter. Forget the TV, that can wait; it will slow you down and sidetrack you from the work that has to be done.

It is always the first act that is the hardest; walking through the door into a small, dusty empty space. It's just an empty canvas awaiting a masterpiece. You will allocate a corner for all the unsorted items, a corner for all the sorted items. In the middle will be piles for everything that's going; you have it in the middle where it will be most in your way to remind you to deal with it. If possible, have someone you trust help you. Make it fun, and make sure you have enough supplies to keep you in hot mugs of tea (in winter) or cold drinks in summer. Make sure you keep your energy up, but take regular breaks so that can review progress. You may need to go out for a walk every so often to get to know your new surroundings and get supplies. Make time to meditate on new possibilities, on your dreams (sustainable ones of course) and on discovering new friends.

If this is a family endeavour you have the added complication of how to maintain morale while dividing the labour. It can be made into a giant game within which everyone has a say. Small children can be the great

distraction as well as being the great joy, keeping you sane through what might be a traumatic event. The reality of many of these downsizing events is that quite often you might be carrying a good deal of anger or guilt about your new situation. You may also be changing employment, or looking for new employment. It is much easier to do either if your home life is settled and happy, much harder if you are living in chaos and squalor. You will have to divide your time between many tasks; some will be simply automatic and physical, others requiring a clearer brain. You will become tired, very tired, and it will be tempting to spend some of your hard earned/hard saved/few remaining funds on alcohol to 'reward' yourself for your endeavours. Everyone knows the effects of alcohol; the first half-teaspoon can be a stimulant, but after that it is a depressive, and of course it is highly addictive. It may be part of the reason why you have come to this place in your life. All drugs are like that; surrender to them and you will never get your life together. The effects are particularly devastating in a family situation, with your children particularly more likely to become addicted and violent if you yourself have not managed to control your demons. The after-effects of alcohol or other drugs will make it harder to get up in the morning and face the tasks ahead of you. If you do drink, then wait until everything's sorted, until then tea will do nicely.

It is fairly obvious that in writing this book I am campaigning for the human population to take up less land for living and leave more land for growing food and for Nature; which keeps us all safe. A growing population with a greater appetite for expansive living (and car parking) means less land for food; which translates into accelerated extinction for humankind. As I watch my children doing their homework next to me I wonder about the world they will inherit, and wonder if I have done enough to give them a sustainable happy life.

The good thing is that everyone knows about sustainability, however not everyone has really assimilated the practical understanding of how to achieve it. Compact living is certainly an important component of a sustainable vision, but it is not the whole thing. One of my sons recently came home with an interesting question to answer in an English essay, which was: 'What Are The Three Most Important Things In The World?'. As usual the boy asked the question of the nearest parent (who happened to be me), and for seemingly no apparent reason I came up with: Love, Soil and Joined-Up Thinking. We then had one of those too-long sessions where the child regrets asking the question while the parent drones on for 20-30mins, holding up supper!

Anyway, I still hold to those three tenets. Love is obvious; it is the most powerful of motivating emotions, it can raise human endeavour to heroic heights, and stay the hand of greed, arrogance and evil (if you believe in it). Soil, because we need it to live. Although it appears to be everywhere underfoot, we barely notice the damage we do to it and the catastrophe that follows when we lose it (and we are losing billions of tonnes and millions of hectares of it every year to urbanisation, deforestation, pollution and bad industrial agricultural practices). Joined-Up Thinking (JUT)? This is what our politicians should be doing, but only pay lipservice to. Permaculture is a prime example of JUT: It centres the mind in seeing the connections between things; it is about balance; the ripple of cause and effect through a system, whether it is food from a landscape or people in a society. When a politician starts talking about sustainable growth (which is a contradiction in terms) or energy security by pumping more oil, you know that it is time to start eating what you grow where you live, and to start looking for new leaders who understand JUT.

Of course, by grasping *Compact Living*, you will have lots more time and energy to build a brighter, more sustainable future for your children and mine.

Thank you for taking the time to read this book.

THE ROOF GARDEN

© Heath Robinson &
K.R.G. Browne

RESOURCES

I'd like to think that this little volume is fairly definitive, and stands all by itself. Of course it isn't. For that reason most 'how-to' books will have an enormous list of other books and publications that you can refer to in order to expand your knowledge. It's quite incestuous actually, and of course other publishers will want you to buy their books, either in physical paper or virtually by download.

Well, I am not going to do that. Publications go out of print, websites change, new manufacturers come and old ones go, new technologies are invented, and so on.

So if you want more information about selling/recycling/archiving/ woodwork/eco-renovation/growing food, etc. find a book that suits your level of knowledge and first borrow them from the library or look through them in a book shop, and if you really like the book then buy it. Look at book reviews on the internet, look at self-help websites (not the ones that want to sell a set of how-to tapes) and the local authority websites (these can really help you with your recycling). Remember that you are not the only person in the world facing a compact future, and that the tools to help you can be found almost anywhere. However, it is best not to spend all your time in libraries, bookshops or on a computer avoiding the real work.

Lastly, enjoy the journey. By having less stuff and a smaller space to look after it in, you ultimately win yourself lower bills, and the opportunity to discern what you really need and what you really want to do with your time and resources. There is nothing quite as liberating as eschewing aspirational normality.

Picture credits: Cover: © Max Topchii/Shutterstock; pp.9, 81, Alexandr Steblovskiy/Fotolia; p.11, Jakub Krechowicz/Fotolia; spiral notebook, pp.23, 45, 46, 80, patpitchaya/Fotolia; pp.30, 68, Coprid/Fotolia; p.31, Sever180/Fotolia; p.41, Svitlana Zaporozhets/Fotolia; p.65, Les Cunliffe/Fotolia; p.84, Elenathewise/ Fotolia; p.100, lucato/iStockphoto.com. Drawings on pages 15, 26, 42, 63, 70, 77, 94 and 105 from *How To Live In A Flat* by Heath Robinson and K.R.G. Browne, first Published (by Hutchinson) 1936, 1976, Duckworth Edition published by Gerald Duckworth & Co. Ltd, The Old Piano Factory, 43 Gloucester Crescent, NW1, ISBN 0 7156 1065 1, used by permission. All other illustrations are the author's copyright.

Inspiration for
Sustainable Living

More books from Permanent Publications

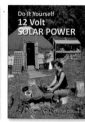

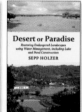

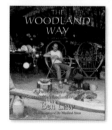

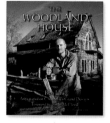

ALL THESE & MORE
AVAILABLE FROM ALL GOOD STORES IN THE ENGLISH SPEAKING WORLD
AND FROM:

www.permanentpublications.co.uk